MONI
SUND

MW01705439

MONDAYS ARE YELLOW, SUNDAYS ARE GREY

WITHDRAWN
LONDON PUBLIC LIBRARIES

ELLEN PRESCOTT

DOUGLAS & McINTYRE
Vancouver/Toronto

Copyright © 1994 by Ellen Prescott

94 95 96 97 98 5 4 3 2 1

All rights reserved. No part of this book may be reproduced in any form by any means without written permission from the publisher, except by a reviewer, who may quote brief passages in a review.

Douglas & McIntyre
1615 Venables Street
Vancouver, British Columbia V5L 2H1

Canadian Cataloguing in Publication Data

Prescott, Ellen, 1954–
Mondays are yellow, Sundays are grey

ISBN 1-55054-121-8

1. Prescott, Ellen, 1954– 2. Incest victims—British Columbia—Biography. 3. Adult child sexual abuse victims—British Columbia—Biography. 4. Sexually abused children—British Columbia. I. Title
HV6570.9CP73 1994 306.877′092 C94-910049-8

Editing by Barbara Pulling
Cover design by Tania Craan
Cover illustration by Pascal Milelli
Text design by Arifin Graham, Alaris Design
Typeset by Brenda and Neil West, Typographics West
Printed and bound in Canada
Printed on acid-free paper ∞

This book is for the women
who work to stop sexual assault

And for Carolina and Amy

Sex is the alibi

Tethered and bound
Our backs across the room
From each other we sing

—OLGA BROUMAS, "THE PROHIBITION"

PROLOGUE

IN 1982, WHEN my daughters were four and one, I decided to kill them.

It was a hot, late June day; in the landlord's garden, blue lupine climbed the garage wall. A dull, rotund cat sun-bathed on the stone fence. It was two o'clock, and there was a humming silence on our quiet East Vancouver street. My children were sleeping, sweetly sleeping, Carolina in her yellow flowered sundress, Amy in only a diaper with the red ribbon from her soother falling across her chest. Both girls slept on their backs with their limbs askew, their hair damp and curled on their brows. Carolina clutched her blanket and Amy, her grey elephant.

I was so in love with them, there at the door of their bedroom, that all I could think of was murder.

I had not folded up my bed yet, and I lurched through the musty basement hallway to the disarray of my sheets. The suite was all of a parcel: I slept alone in the living room, which adjoined the ungenerous kitchen. I stripped off my robe and crawled into bed, wrapping humidly around myself.

My thoughts were in a formative language, a language without letters. Just one thing was clear: I *must* kill Carolina and Amy. I considered drowning them, how hard it would be to hold Amy and still compel Carolina to walk with me into the cold ocean water.

I took the girls to the beach as often as I could, with their plastic buckets and shovels and day-old bread for the gulls and ducks. I never tired of watching them out of doors, their adorable, still-creased legs, their fascination with castles and muck. How large the world must seem, I thought as I sat watching them and smoking, my back up against a log, the mountains blue and hazy across the inlet. Dogs were big to Carolina and Amy, and so were cats. Even the greedy, swooping gulls were big. I was big. Someday, I thought, they will think of me as small. Like everything, this will be a discovery. For the first time, two months earlier, Amy had said Mama. For the first time, two weeks before, Carolina had flushed a grown-up toilet. I tried to understand the experience they were having, this theatre curtain rising, this heart-stopping adventure called childhood.

If I had a gun, would I shoot them? That would at least be fast. I wondered if I would have the courage: could I look at Amy, curly-haired Amy with her luminous blue eyes, with her legs kicking in her crib, and shoot her? Point blank? That body, those bodies I grew so enthusiastically inside my own, those luscious small bodies, Carolina's little toes and spatulate fingers, her toss of black hair?

When Carolina was almost nine months old, after she had crawled for only two weeks, she began to walk. It was Christmas Day, 1978. She wore a smocked dress of robin's egg blue my mother had sent from Arizona, white tights and no shoes. We were in her bedroom, all of us, me and her father, Frank, too, showing her multisized coloured rings that slid onto a tube, when Carolina began to catapult from me to her father, giggling and tilting drastically forward, two steps then four then eight, her momentum finally cascading her into her daddy's arms in a wild peal of laughter. From then on, Carolina walked everywhere. When we went along the city streets to shop, she would toddle beside me, clutching my hand, improbably propelling herself along. I'd walk bent because she was so very short. She was a baby, very nearly an infant, but she was walking, and also talking articulately, in sentences. People stopped to stare.

Everything Carolina did was a sort of miracle to me. Living with her was living in a brilliant maze of miracles, turning every corner to find a new delight, a surprise, a rapture.

Pills are the thing, I thought all of a sudden. The realization was as hot as the mean June afternoon, there in my bed: pills, yes, whatever sorts of pills killed. Barbiturates. I could put powder into ice cream; I could lie us down in my big bed and hold the girls tight, and we could drift off to a game of Itsy Bitsy Spider, to Raffi on the tape deck.

Something loosened inside me. I slept.

I didn't know why I wanted to kill my kids. I knew it arose from instinct, that I felt like a cornered animal, fiercely protective. That murdering them, annihilating them, was a thought both unbearable and unbearably sweet in its release. This was our den; even holed up in it, though, we were still not safe. *They* were not safe. Carolina and Amy were in utter jeopardy. I knew that as thoroughly as I knew my name. It was knowledge that had been growing in increments since before Amy's birth, gaining momentum until now, nearly three months after my separation from Frank, it was at fever pitch. The girls were in trouble.

The problem was, on that Wednesday late in June, I didn't know why. I only registered the threat as it swelled towards them like fire, pressing its vivid story. I only knew I had to save my daughters, that saving them was more important to me than breath.

And so, I should kill them.

PART ONE

1

"WHAT'RE YOU DOING?" I whispered.

"Shh," said Frank.

I heard a wrinkle of foil. The darkness was total, and though I tried hard to make him out, I couldn't see a thing. I had to rely on other senses, touch and smell. I wasn't used to having sex without light. Frank had tugged his jeans off while he lay on his back, then reached for me, pulling me up a crude ladder and under a heavy down sleeping bag. It was awkward, close; the ceiling was only three feet above his elevated bed. We kissed. I began to stroke his shoulders and arms. He was muscular from farm work and smelled faintly of what I took to be straw; I felt the stirrings of arousal.

Frank turned away from me slightly, and I fanned small kisses across his back. "Wait," he said. "Ellen, shit, wait a minute."

Finally I figured out what he was doing. He was rolling on a condom.

Perplexed, I told him I was on the pill.

He rolled back to face me. "Women give me infections."

"What?" I said. "What are you talking about?"

"C'mere," he said and pulled me to him. He kissed me and touched my breasts very softly. Then he entered me and ejaculated.

Frank Moore was lovely to look at. A photographer and silver-smith who earned his living training horses, he was tall and thin with long, shocked black hair. His blue-green eyes were sleepy and blank, which made him seem mysterious. His body was perfect. He wore jeans and western flannel shirts. He hardly ever talked, and when he did it was with a sort of southern drawl, as if he were pulling words through molasses.

It was early 1977. I was twenty-two, passing through Vancouver to stay with my brother Laurence en route from New York to San Francisco, and after two days in town I'd looked Frank up. We had dated for a short time in high school, and whatever had attracted me to him then—I'd never been able to quite pinpoint it—was still there five years later. Frank was a magnet; I was the iron shavings we'd pushed around on our school desktops. Once as teen-agers we were driving down Strawberry Street, rounding a curve, when Frank, sadness rasping his voice, whispered, "I'd like to kill myself." He almost ditched us, but his words caused an answering hammer to bang in my chest. I hadn't known what to say. It made me see him as dangerous and romantic.

These days Frank was a hippie, sort of. After being at university in fast-paced Manhattan, I found Frank's slow, semi-rural lifestyle appealing; it seemed like a kind of oasis. I postponed my trip south, an easy decision. I wasn't heading to San Francisco for any particular reason, just as somewhere to go after graduation. I had a degree in psychology and one practicum working with autistic kids, but I wasn't sure what I wanted to do next.

Frank was drifting too. He didn't seem to have aspirations except for his photography—he hoped one day to be good enough to have a show. I didn't doubt he would. He had real talent. He showed me how to handle myself in a darkroom, but his talent was something I didn't share: an ability to find a meaningful juxtaposition of light, subject and shadow. By the time I wondered if I was in love with him, I was just as much in love with the pictures he took. And with British Columbia's scenery. Frank and I spent long days hiking up the sides of snow-capped mountains and along stretches of beach and ocean. I felt safe, at peace.

One morning when I awoke beside Frank a pungent odour assailed me. I knew at once it was urine. I moved against the sheet—wet. I reached down to touch my legs—wet. I'd wet the bed every night of my life till I was thirteen, and now, after a ten-year break, I'd done it again. I lay stone cold quiet against Frank, more ashamed than I could stand.

When Frank came to, he blinked into the light. He moved sleepily, adjusting his position, and I watched his even features blur with confusion when he realized he was wet.

Tentatively, I stroked his cheek. "I'm sorry," I whispered.

"What's going on?" he asked.

Oh God, I thought, make me die. I didn't know how to move an explanation through my humiliation. I whispered so low he had to crane to hear. "It was me. I had ... an accident."

"Did you—?"

I nodded frantically to interrupt him, then jerked away and started down the ladder. "I'm sorry," I told him again. I felt the chill morning air touch my damp skin.

Frank was frowning. It's coming now, I thought with dread. He'll kick me out and never want to see me again.

Instead, he backed down the ladder after me. He took my elbow gently, steering me towards the bathroom. "Let's have a shower," he said.

"You don't mind?"

He shook his head and shrugged. "I have six brothers and sisters, Ellen. Don't worry about it."

I was so grateful I hardly knew what to do.

≈

1963

"Ellen," a voice says. A whisper that I climb to out of sleep.

"Mommy?"

"Ellen," my mother repeats harshly. "Jill said, Wake Ellen. Ellen'll know what to do. I'm waking up Ellen now. She's my daughter."

It's the middle of the night, a time I've scarcely seen before at nine years old. Pulling up into the dark, I prop myself on my elbows.

"See? I have a knife. Ellen, this is a knife from the kitchen. You know this knife, don't you?"

My mother smells sour. There is enough moonlight to see that she wears a bra and is otherwise naked, enough to memorize the shape of the knife that she raises over me. I do know it. It's our roast-beef knife.

"Ellen will know what to do."

"Mommy?"

She turns and pads out of my room, buttocks puddling, feet squeaking over the boards in the hall.

I follow her. "Mommy, what's wrong? Please, Mommy, please say."

She's in bed when I reach her room. Everything is woozy, without definition. There is Mom's bed, all right; there are her sheets and blankets in a hump, there's Mom with the big knife, but it's like looking at things under water. She smells like diarrhea. She pulls the knife to her chest and curls around it.

"I'm going to kill myself," she says, but now her voice becomes happy and sweet, very different from her mean whisper in my room. A bird-song voice. She adds, "Call your father. Call the doctor, Ellen. Call Dr. Thomas. Better hurry."

She lifts the knife, stares at it and giggles. She says, "Oops."

"Mommy, how?" Daddy has moved out. I don't know how to call him or the doctor.

There's a large silence. I can feel urine falling down my leg. Not a big, bathroom burst of it, but a trickle.

My mother looks at me. A normal look. She frowns and says, "Look the doctor's number up, Ellen. Don't you know anything?"

She has a metal directory on her bedside table. I pull my eyes from her, move the indicator to T, push the button.

"Phone! Telephone! Microphone! Gramophone! Ellen is on the gramophone."

"What do I say?" My hands are flopping all around, won't stay still. I lift the heavy black receiver—it's stone cold—and dial. My finger keeps falling out of the holes.

"Tell him," my mother says, her voice gone deep, "tell him your mother's about to commit suicide."

When a woman answers—I didn't know it wouldn't be Dr. Thomas—I give a little cry of shock.

"Yes? Dr. Thomas's answering service. Is someone there?"

"It's me," I say, my voice rubbery. I reach down and hold my crotch.

"Speak up. Who is this? Are you playing games?"

She's mad.

I use Mom's words, thick on my tongue. "My mother's about to ... to uh ... commit suicide."

She gets even madder. "Who is this? Do I know you? What's your name?"

"Is this Dr. Thomas?" I feel stupid. I know she isn't Dr. Thomas. Dr. Thomas is a man.

"Dr. Thomas is out of town. Dr. Moore is on call. Tell me your name."

I look at my mother. She has the tip of the knife just above the top of her bra, poking at her skin, denting it. "She has a big knife."

"I need to know your name and address so Dr. Moore can come and help you. Tell me your name."

"Ellen."

"Your last name?"

"Billings," I say. "It's really big."

"What's big?"

"It's very big. The knife is big. My mother is crying." She isn't. I am. I'm not making any sound, but tears are sneaking into my mouth.

"Where do you live?"

"In Burlington."

"On what street?"

"Maple." She doesn't like me.

"What's your number on Maple?"

I tell her our phone number.

"Your street number."

"One-eighteen," I say.

"Hang up now. Are you listening, Ellen? Hang up now. Are you upstairs?"

"Yes."

"Go downstairs and unlock the door for the doctor. You're a brave little girl. Can you do that for me?"

I nod.

"Ellen?"

"Yes."

"Do that now, please. Hang up and go wait for the doctor."

There's a big thunk as I put the receiver back. It's a very heavy telephone.

"Well?" says my mother.

"I have to go downstairs and unlock the door," I tell her, jiggling my hand in my crotch so no more pee can come out.

"Well, go then," she says.

I've never been downstairs in the dark before. I'm sure it's wrong to go now, because my mother has a knife. I'm very slow. I touch the wall all the way down the stairs. In the foyer I start hugging myself and I can feel goose bumps. "Nice house," I say, starting forward. "Good house. Nice, good house." I creep under the chandelier, past the gaping hole of the basement stairs into the kitchen. "Nice table. Nice chairs. Nice counter." I slide my way past the glubbing freezer to the back entrance hall, past the coats on pegs that I think might grab me. There's the back door. I reach up to unlock it.

"Uh oh," I say. My voice sounds like the freezer, all shaky. "Robbers might get in. Robbers are bad."

I know I have to stay put. Or else. I stand on my tiptoes and part the drapes to watch the driveway for car lights. I plan that when I see lights I'll quick unlock the door.

"Bad old robbers. Don't move one inch. Hurry up, Mr. Doctor. Hurry up if you know what's good for you."

I forget it's not Dr. Thomas coming. This doctor has on a big grey coat. He smells like snow. He has galoshes on. He has a black bag.

"I'm Dr. Moore. Are you the girl who called?" he says in a gruff voice.

I shrink back into the coats. Nod my head.

"Where's your mother?"

"Up," I whisper.

"Where?"

I point.

"Go back to bed," he says and reaches to touch my hair. "Your mother's going to be fine now. Your mother will be all better in the morning."

≈

Frank and I spent most of our time together when he wasn't at work. One early spring day he asked if I'd like to go riding. I was excited. I'd ridden a lot when I was small, on the hobby farm just northwest of Burlington, Ontario, where my parents had raised hunters, jumpers and Shetland ponies.

The horses were good ones, not rentals. Frank gave me a leg up onto my mare. It was western saddle, new for me, so Frank explained how I should sit, how to hold the reins and use the saddle horn. I was glad to find that the rest came back to me. Frank led us out on a slow walk. I felt confident, and I found myself mesmerized by the slow and even rhythm of the mare's flanks. When Frank galloped, leading along a forest trail, and my horse galloped after, my body knew those rhythms, too, how to control her, how to ride smoothly.

Frank pulled in his horse at a small clearing surrounded by fir trees. After helping me dismount, he produced a bottle of wine and a knapsack from his saddlebag.

"You're kidding," I said. "You made us a picnic?"

He snapped a blue and white checked tablecloth over the grass, then set out two juice glasses and a corkscrew. While I stood gawking, my thighs sore and trembling from the ride, he unwrapped sandwiches and a plastic container filled with cookies. It was cool, and I sat down gingerly, feeling the wet grass soak through the tablecloth and my jeans.

Frank filled our glasses. "To us," he said, smiling.

I nodded. "To us," I repeated. I wasn't used to drinking, so I sipped my wine slowly.

I leaned in against his shoulder. He told me he loved me, that he'd loved me since high school. He said he wanted to be with me forever.

I was taken aback. Frank and I were definitely an item, but he still had a girlfriend in a nearby town. I'd never met her, but I'd been jealous of her since the beginning, and I resented the fact that Frank wasn't mine alone. I hadn't been able to pin him down on which one of us he wanted.

I wasn't sure if I loved Frank, but I liked him, and I liked the life he offered me. He had a large circle around him, people as easygoing as he was. They were artists, a lot of them, sculptors and poets and painters and dancers. I was the sort of woman who latched on to one special friend, but Frank had lots of friends. He wasn't close to his friends in the way I was to mine, but people gravitated to him. I couldn't really figure it out—he didn't actively do anything to maintain these friendships, and he was too quiet to be called charming. Yet his phone rang constantly. I wanted some of that to rub off on me. Plus I wanted him to give up that damned girlfriend.

Frank reached for an egg salad sandwich. "Move in with me," he said.

"Really?" My heart was pounding.

"Call your friend in San Francisco and get him to send up your things."

"Are you sure, Frank? God, it's a big move."

"Have a sandwich," he said.

≈

1972

Frank Moore wants to cheat. We're studying revolutions. All I can think of when I think of revolutions is a song by the Beatles. I hate history. But I'm way better at it than Frank. I slide my test papers over to the edge of my desk so he can copy the answers. He's already been kept back once; this year he'll graduate. Except for wanting my test answers, I don't think he even knows I'm alive.

Until one Wednesday when he walks me out of the classroom. I can't believe it. He's one of the popular boys. He was Carie Andrews's boyfriend and she's the most beautiful girl in the school. Now he's slouched against the row of lockers, inviting me, in his slow, almost paralytic way, to a party Saturday night. I shrug and say, "Sure," as if it doesn't matter, but my heart's knocking halfway to hell.

I'm scared because he's one of Dr. Moore's kids. Because he's Catholic. Because he doesn't care about anything. And because he comes from a normal family.

I don't want him to find out too much about me. I don't want him to know that my mother's addicted to prescription drugs, or that some of her prescriptions have his father's name on the bottles. When my mother's doped up, or even more frequently when she stops cold turkey, she slurs at me, calling me a slut.

I keep razor blades between my mattresses. In case I need to die. And I don't want Frank Moore to find out.

≈

A couple of days after our picnic, Frank asked me to go off the pill. He was worried about me ingesting the chemicals. "What'll I use?" I asked him. He was working at his desk, bent into the light of a gooseneck lamp, using a blowtorch to twist the handle of a spoon into a ring. He laid the torch aside and pulled off a pair of protective glasses.

"Nothing," he said, a kind of challenge.

"What about Michelle?" I asked.

"If you go off the pill," Frank said, his lips pulling up at the corners in a kind of half grin, "I'll stop seeing her. I'll tell her it's over."

I cleared my throat. "Frank, are you telling me you want to have a baby? I don't even know if I'm staying in Canada."

"Don't you want to stay? What can I do to convince you?"

Frank turned to his desk, picked up the ring he'd been working on and gestured for me to get up. He patted his knee. He held up my left hand and slipped the ring onto it. It was clunky, still faintly warm from the fire.

"Frank, do you mean it? I can go off the pill?" I wanted to ask him about getting married, but I knew he didn't believe in it. I guessed I didn't really believe in it either.

I'd discarded my New York wardrobe for billowing cotton dresses and small black ballet slippers. I no longer fixed my hair or wore make-up. I'd always been scared of lots of things, but with Frank I felt safe. I was home.

Things were good, good enough. I'd been at loose ends, not knowing what to do with my life, and Frank held just enough of me in his hands to keep me beside him. I asked my friend in San Francisco to mail my things north.

2

AT THE DOCTOR'S OFFICE, I crackled through my symptoms. I vomited, I said, without warning and for no apparent reason. I'd be at home or over at a friend's house when all of a sudden my throat would open and huck would race up and out, flying two or three feet.

She nodded and scratched a note.

"Do you think it's cancer?"

"Pop up on the table," she said. "Are you tired?"

"Waking up is a chore," I confirmed. She prodded my face and throat and stomach.

"Breasts sore?" she asked, moving them back and forth in her hands like balls. "Any enlargement, tenderness?"

"Yes," I said.

"When did you last have your period?"

"The end of June."

She stuck gloved fingers inside me and palpated my uterus. Then she drew out her hand and grinned over my knees. "Best I can tell, Ellen, you're six to eight weeks pregnant."

I sat up quickly, delighted, propping myself on my elbows.

"Congratulations," the doctor said.

After a blood test confirmed the doctor's suspicion, I rushed home with a box of cigars. "Congratulations," I said, passing one to Frank, holding out my lighter. "You're going to be a daddy."

Slowly, very slowly, without registering emotion, Frank stripped the plastic off the cigar, bit its end and put it to his lips.

"So?" I said, "so?" I was wobbly with happiness, though the news was still sinking in, but worried, too. Would he want it? It wasn't exactly an accident, but it was unexpected. "Is that … okay? Are you happy?"

Cigar fumes billowed out. I coughed and backed away. My father had smoked cigars; the smell made me ill. I swallowed hard.

"Ellen," Frank finally said with his eyes sparking and a curious smile lifting his lips, "that's great. That's just great."

Frank closed his eyes, leaned back and contentedly puffed on his cigar. I looked hard at him, frozen in place as cold chills prickled up my arms, raising the hairs. His smile was giving me the creeps. It looked eerily familiar but I couldn't think from where. It was August and hot, but there in our kitchen I hugged myself, rubbing my hands up and down the goose-pimpled flesh of my arms. For a second, I was pregnant and sorry.

≈

1971

I didn't mean to get pregnant. I guess I know I am; I miss two periods in a row. But the thought is like a penny on the bottom of a swimming pool, barely visible, and by the time I tell my mother, I'm nearly three months along.

Mom doesn't get upset. She's very sanguine about it. We talk about my options and she advises an abortion.

A pregnant girl has to see three doctors and convince them that her health will be endangered if she maintains the pregnancy. I'll kill myself before I'll be an unwed mother; I have no trouble telling the doctors so.

I'm dirty. I'm seventeen, humiliated. I tell no one but Mom. Not my best girlfriend, Peggy, and not my boyfriend, Martin.

In the course of examining me, the doctors find what they think is cancer. They run tests.

My mother and I have a blow-out.

"They say you won't be able to have more kids, Ellen. You have *to keep this baby."*

"Lay off, Mom. I do goddamned not."

"Listen to me, Ellen." She grabs my shoulders. "You don't understand what it'll be like. You don't understand it's a whole life. It doesn't mean anything to you now, but when you're twenty-five, thirty, you're going to want a baby so much."

I twist away. "Drop dead, Mom," I say, tears whipping free. "You can't make me keep it."

By the time they figure out I have absolutely nothing wrong with me, it's too late to have a first trimester abortion. I'm secreted in a hospital for a saline one, on a maternity ward. Alone, on the toilet, I give birth to a dead, five-month-old foetus.

At school after my abortion, memories of how the dead baby dangled between my legs flash during history class, and my breasts spurt milk.

No one told me that my breasts would spill milk, that my blouses would soak through with everyone watching.

Maybe everyone knows; I was at school the whole time I was pregnant. I gained weight and suddenly lost it. But there seems to be an unspoken pact: no one, friend or enemy, mentions it.

≈

Frank and I rented a bungalow in a quiet neighbourhood. The house had dark, oily plywood walls that gave the rooms a cavernous glow, but it also had hardwood floors, a screened sun porch, two bedrooms and a partially renovated basement. Someone had left a maroon overstuffed couch and chair behind, and we needed them; besides Frank's bed, which I asked him to cut down so that I wouldn't have to manoeuvre a ladder, we had no furniture. Still, I'd acquired a jungle of houseplants and box after box of books and dishes, enough to start us off, and we scrounged the rest. Outside in the weedy garden patch, I sunk spring bulbs, crocuses and daffodils and tulips I hoped might bloom by the time the baby came.

The baby was everything to me. I'd already decided that she'd be a girl and that her name would be Carolina. I tried to imagine her there in my belly: how large she was, what her stage of development. I borrowed books from the library and bought others. I read them while I ate crackers and small tubs of fruited yogurt that Frank sweetly ran out to buy: I couldn't learn or eat enough. Mornings I preened, longing to see myself show, longing to see Carolina in a mirror. My reflection, though, displayed only the flat and unremarkable belly I had once dieted and exercised into just that shape.

By October, just after our move, I was into my second trimester. The morning sickness was gone. The baby, who apparently looked like a small, translucent alien, would soon grow large enough for me to detect her movements.

One night Frank and I were sitting on our couch when I felt Carolina kick. I had the tiniest pot belly, of which I was inordinately proud. I felt a small, determined thunk, bigger than a gas bubble, right under my navel. I grinned, shot through with a quick dose of pleasure, and speedily unzipped my pants. "Frank," I said, "Frank!" I slouched down and put my hands against my skin.

Frank looked embarrassed. "Ellen," he said, "do up your pants." He took a toke on the joint he was smoking.

"No, Frank, no. I can feel the baby. I can *feel* it. It's kicking me, Frank."

I reached for his hand but he pulled away. "Ellen, I'm getting the camera."

"The camera?" I said. Frank bewildered me. He wouldn't show much interest in my pregnancy and then, all at once, he'd want to take pictures. He'd photographed me the day I announced I was pregnant and again the day we moved into the house. The pictures were in a special album; arrows in black felt pen pointed to my belly and announced "Baby!" Partly I thought it was sweet, this urge of his, but partly I felt uncomfortable. "Goddamn it," I said, but then Carolina began a series of collisions with my stomach that scooped my attention. There she was, burbling and popping inside me, my little salmon, my little dolphin, jumping through hoops.

When Frank developed the pictures, they showed me slovenly on the sofa, not apparently pregnant, and were completely unflattering except for the expression on my face, which was rapt.

I wanted a window into my uterus. How was the baby situated? Where was her head? How much conversation could she hear? Did she hear my voice from the inside out, but others' voices only indistinctly? She certainly, I thought, could not smell, which required air, and could not taste—or did she taste the umbilical waters? Did she see, and if so, what? The watery pink of floating tissues? Did she suck her thumb? Most of all, could my thoughts and feelings transfer to her? In 1977, this was a radical question, one my doctor rolled her eyes at. Could I give birth to an optimist by thinking only hopeful thoughts? A depressive if I schlumped around? A hard worker if I was industrious?

Frank and I set to work renovating Carolina's room. The walls were lumpy with layers of wallpaper; these we stripped, peeling them away in long, ragged gashes. After fifteen layers, we came, finally, to wood slats. Frank and his friends Steve and Mark, and sometimes his brother Dennis, drywalled, manoeuvring huge sheets of wallboard through the door, then cutting, nailing and taping. I began to paper in a white and floral print. I painted the woodwork soft pink. Frank and I bought a green carpet. When we were through, the room, transformed, looked exactly like spring. Carolina was due the first week of April.

Our families had greeted the announcement of my pregnancy with mostly unspoken concern. Since Dr. Moore and Frank's mom, Mary (I was to call her Mary), were back east and my mother and sister lived in Arizona, where my mother had moved to care for her aging father years before, there wasn't much they could do.

Over the phone, Frank's family acted friendly and warm, and I was grateful. The shame of what Dr. Moore had witnessed when I was young rolled soft and oily inside me, but I pushed aside my queasiness about it. No one referred back to that earlier encounter; I hoped I was forgiven my mother. Frank's parents seemed glad to see their son finally settling down even if, in the style of the day, we weren't marrying. One of his sisters had had a child while unmarried; maybe his parents were getting used to it.

In any case, I thought that over time Frank and I would show them what an upstanding respectable couple we were. We'd have a perfect family—just like theirs, solid, stable and wholesome.

≈

1958

My mother lets herself out of my brother's room. Laurence may be asleep, but I'm not. My mother's been reading Laurence Now We Are Six *by A.A. Milne and I'm jealous. I want her to read this book to* me, *and I'm out of bed, just about to call to her across the hall, when I notice my father.*

He stands down the hallway at the door to my parents' room, about ten feet away. In his raised hands is a rifle. He cocks it.

I watch, hidden behind my door.

My mother begins to beg. "Please, Mike," she says, "not here. Not here with the kids."

She's whispering.

But my father isn't listening. His face, always ruddy, is beet red.

My mother says, "Please take me outside. Where the kids won't see."

Silence falls. I don't move. I try not to breathe.

Perspiration breaks out on my father's forehead. My mother carefully pulls Laurence's door closed behind her, then stands quietly watching my father.

At last she edges towards him. They've been at the country club for dinner. He's wearing his best pair of slacks. "Mike," she says quietly, "if you shoot me, you'll get blood on your good pants."

My father frowns and looks down. When he sees she is right, he lowers the rifle.

≈

There was much to arrange. I'd decided to give birth to Carolina at home, and so, besides the usual accoutrements gathered for a newborn—the crib, the mobile, the clothes, the diapers, the change table, the cradle, the rocking chair, the formula, the toys—I had also to gather home birthing supplies. Frank was aghast. He wanted me to go to a hospital; I flatly refused. He spoke to his father, who spoke to me; he pleaded and even once hollered, but I was resolute. Carolina would be born calmly, into the bosom of her family, with those who loved her at her side, where I could take her to my breast.

Frank, I thought, was only scared, so I did my best to educate him, showing him books, reading him statistics, pointing out the benefits to Carolina of being born in a natural setting. He stopped trying to talk me out of it and went silent. His silence served my purpose and my preoccupation so I ignored it, took it to be a kind of assent. It meant one thing to me, really: relief. Frank wasn't going to get in my way.

I bought sheets that I sterilized in a brown paper bag in the oven. I bought a suction device, surgical gloves and shoelaces to tie off Carolina's umbilical cord. The list of supplies was two pages long. I found a doctor who would attend a home birth; my new friend Ruby, with whom I spent long, fat hours playing Rummy 500, agreed to act as a labour coach.

Frank and I signed up for prenatal classes. Once a week, come December, he and I trundled off to the basement rec room of a woman named Debbie, and with other couples learned how to breathe. We learned to pant and push. We watched a movie of a baby being born and Frank felt faint.

"It's like a well," Frank said stubbornly later when we were in bed.

I said he was silly. Vaginas were not wells. "A well implies it goes on forever."

"Sometimes I think I'll push out your mouth."

"You can't get lost in me," I said. Pregnant, I wanted more sex than he did. I knew perfectly well I didn't get what I needed—what did I need? Orgasms?—from making love with Frank, but I was still always after him. No foreplay? Premature ejaculation? Sex that as often as not left me cold? Didn't matter. I wanted more of it. I stroked down his chest to his belly.

"Ellen, no," he said. "What if I hurt the baby?"

"You're overestimating yourself."

Frank was hurt and turned away. I curled up behind him, apologizing over and over again, but he was stiff.

"You smell," he finally said.

I turned my back and left him alone.

Pregnancy is an infinitude. Any fool can say it is only nine months, but any pregnant woman knows better. Pregnancy does not end. Pregnancy is a lifetime, and each day within it has the scope of a year. A pregnant woman has always been and will always be with child. She imagines the day this enormous belly will turn itself inside out, dislodging its resident through a passage not much wider than a pencil; this she rolls her mind around, even while, contrary to all opinion, she knows it is impossible.

The last month was the longest haul. I was elephantine. I was twenty-five pounds heavier than in June. I felt like lead. My sciatic nerve sent pains shooting down my left leg. If I went outside when it was cold, my breasts burned so badly I'd race inside, throw off my top and dump them in a sink of hot water. My belly was taut as a drum. I could feel parts of Carolina distinctly: the globe of her head, the foot she nestled above my rib cage under my right breast, cutting off my blood supply and numbing my skin. I waddled. My feet were so swollen they looked like water bottles. Raising myself from a chair took perseverance—I had to really want to stand.

The daffodils I'd planted for Carolina were already dying, their yellow heads shrinking and sagging in the garden. The tulips were robustly in bloom.

Finally, at ten o'clock one Saturday morning, I felt my first cramp. It was so mild, so similar to the minor tugs I experienced with periods, that I wasn't at all certain it was labour. But in its unconvinced way it continued, until by the early afternoon contractions came at timed, ten-minute intervals. Frank and I had tickets to see the Rolling Stones. He was insistent: Could we or couldn't we attend? I kept telling him I didn't know.

At three we walked slowly through the streets of town. I'd read that walking could sometimes bring on stronger contractions, and felt like walking anyway, for something to do.

The day was startlingly bright and warm. Frank put his palm under my elbow and steered me past budding chestnuts and neighbours' flower beds. The forsythia, with their yellow suns, were already gone, as were my favourites, the cherry blossoms, but I saw hyacinths, and aubrieta falling over stone fences in cascades of white and purple.

We stopped at Safeway. Frank carried his grandfather's pocket watch in his hand, and as we wheeled our cart up and down the shiny aisles, he timed my now stronger pains. They were still semi-regular, still moderately spaced and less than a minute long. We picked up groceries: cereal, yogurt, milk and ingredients I needed to make a rice casserole for dinner. I thought it was a remarkable thing to be shopping while I was in labour, and I kept watching other shoppers, wishing they knew. The contractions grew sharper, painful, so that surprised "Oh"s popped from my throat. My hand, as it had for months now, rotated over my belly soothing Carolina. I could feel a change during contractions; my belly seized, then squeezed and felt like stone, hard and dense.

I was able to cook dinner, call our birth attendants and ready the supplies. I had to stop, completely stop, only during the increasingly strong pains. I asked Frank to give away the concert tickets; I asked him to rub my lower back while I hung over the table propping myself on my hands, hurting and blowing.

At nine, our friends Ruby and Mark arrived. The doctor came and examined me, saying I was only three centimetres dilated; I wouldn't give birth, she thought, for another twenty-four hours. But it was starting to hurt terribly. I couldn't do another day, I thought, not without drugs. Not medicinal teas and popsicles—Valium. I asked the doctor, but she just grinned and sat down for tea before leaving.

Suddenly the pain unstrung me. I rode a log through rapids, weeping, a fury of serpents loosed inside. Life was all disaster, all hurricane and tornado. I didn't know my way. I felt my birth helpers like bugs around me, swarms of gnats or mosquitoes, pressing their thin mouths through my skin. I could not speak to tell them to leave me alone.

At ten, Frank dropped implements into a pot of boiling water. Ruby stripped our bed and replaced the sheets. Vaguely, I watched this activity. I didn't really understand what it was for. For the past hour I had been having one single contraction, no breaks, no moment to catch my breath, to speak, to say, Please, what are you all doing here?

Mark manoeuvred me to bed. Someone—Ruby—rolled socks over my feet. Frank crawled in behind me like a hammock. I heard voices as if they came from behind windows: Ellen, roll over on your back so I can check you. Ellen, honey, remember your breathing. Ellen, pant, sugar, c'mon, pant. Ellen, Ellen!

My waters broke. It was a relief, very warm and comforting. Ruby tugged at my socks. I couldn't tell her that wet, they were perfect. An urge to push tore through me. I rolled my shoulders forward, hunched over and grabbed my knees to pull my thighs to my breasts. I gulped air, pushed with my face, my shoulders, my arms, my back and then, finally, at last, my uterus. Frank, behind me, rolled me forward, held me in place. I grunted, lips curled back over clamped teeth. Frank shouted, "Be quiet!" and I heard the doctor scold him. Push, I heard. Push! Ruby and Mark held my legs up, so I grabbed Frank's upper arms and dug in, dug down, all feral, all wild with intent. Growling sow sounds fell from my mouth.

Push! Push! All these urgent voices, hands clamping me hard. An alarmed chorus. I caught their anxious tone and pushed with all my goddamned might, like shoving a haystack through a needle.

The baby's head popped out. I felt it, a sudden release, hugely satisfying, like expelling a bowling ball. I reached down and touched, so I would be first. Someone yelled the time: 10:57! The baby's head rotated. I felt it rotate, the movement against my skin.

Then a new surge swept over me. The doctor's back was turned but I pushed hugely, magnificently, all muscle and impulse.

"Dr. McLaughlin!" I heard Ruby yell, and the doctor turned just quickly enough to grab the squirting baby.

"11:03!" Mark shouted.

I fell back exhausted. Waveringly, I saw the baby in Dr. McLaughlin's arms, the long coil of the blue and white umbilical cord. It was Carolina, at last. I waited for her to cry and when I heard a slight noise of protest, when I saw her turn from a beigy blue to a bright pink, I relaxed. The doctor didn't need to suction her. She passed her to my breast. Frank slid out from behind me; Ruby crammed pillows in where he'd been. Carolina was at my breast, her eyes fastened on my face. Her head rooted, turning from side to side, a little eager shake towards my nipple. She smelled like ocean. She was covered by white patches of vernix; on her mostly bald head was a black tuft of hair. Her features were very delicate and petite. I held my breast, guiding the nipple to her mouth, but she couldn't seem to grasp it. She made tiny mewing sounds of frustration. She'd grab it, finally, then lose it. Dr. McLaughlin cut the cord. Carolina and I were unbound at a snip of the scissors.

Ruby said, "Oh, Ellen, why did you push?"

Dr. McLaughlin laughed. "I almost didn't get my hands under her in time! But you tore yourself, Ellen!"

"I tore?" I said.

"Everyone was yelling, 'Don't push,'" Ruby said.

I grinned sheepishly. "I heard 'push.'" At Ruby's skeptical look I added, "Honest."

Ruby held Carolina while I delivered the afterbirth and while I was sutured. "Ellen," she whispered, "she's so beautiful. Look what you've done."

I did look. I couldn't stop looking. I kept reaching out to stroke her. When Dr. McLaughlin was finished and she took Carolina from the room to weigh her, I couldn't bear being separated from her, so I got out of bed and followed. I was very weak. I walked cautiously, woozily, towards my daughter.

I sagged into the big, overstuffed chair. The doctor put liniment on Carolina's umbilicus and ointment in her eyes. Ruby left to change the linen on our bed. Dr. McLaughlin told me Carolina's Apgar scores—nine and ten—and her weight—seven pounds, two ounces. Finally she let me hold her.

I coaxed Carolina to suckle, gently rubbing the tip of my finger on her cheek. I felt her toes, her feet, her little legs and her flaccid bottom; I was learning her by touch. She suckled, finally. I felt a movement in my breasts that began at my shoulders and a rippling, painful sensation in my nipples. But within a minute, Carolina's eyelids dropped and she lost contact. It was midnight.

Frank carried his camera in. I wanted something from him, some intimacy, and looked imploringly at him.

"Mark and I went out for a cigarette," he said. "Do up your robe, Ellen, all right? I want to get some pictures."

I was throbbing from having been torn and stitched, and I ignored him. Carolina cuddled in my arms. Her eyelashes, black and lush like Frank's, settled on tiny pink cheeks. Her lips were a small bow. Her nose was no bigger than the end of my thumb.

Dr. McLaughlin packed her supplies to go. Frank messed with camera gear. Carolina was still naked under a receiving blanket. It was very hot in the house since we'd bumped the thermostat to ninety-five for the birth. I kept drawing bits of the blanket aside to marvel at Carolina's shoulders and her fat, creased arms, to smooth the birth vernix into her skin.

The doctor said she'd call in the morning. She wanted me to bring Carolina to her office every three days for the first two weeks. She took my hand and kissed my forehead. "You did a wonderful job."

I smiled up at her. "Thank you," I said. "Thank you very much."

"Call me if there's anything," Dr. McLaughlin said. "Any time of the day or night."

"Of course." I beamed.

"Frank," she said, "help me out to the car with these things."

Reluctantly, Frank lowered his camera.

Ruby sat with me. Carolina woke and snuffled in to nurse. I was surprised. She was like a little cougar, very fierce. I laughed and tried to help her, but as soon as she was attached and nursing, causing the stir through my breasts, she fell fast asleep again.

"It must have been hard work for her, too," Ruby said.

"I wonder what it's like to feel air on her skin? What's it like to breathe?" We heard the kitchen door open, male voices.

"She didn't cry," Ruby said. She turned away, watched Mark and Frank across the room light a joint.

"Toke?" Mark asked, but Ruby shook her head.

"Do you want anything, Ellen?" Ruby said. "Juice or tea?"

"Juice, sure," I said. "And a diaper." Carolina had just wet.

Frank was back at the camera, but he frowned when he saw Carolina on my breast. She hadn't broken the suction; every few seconds her jaws started working, though not strongly enough to pull milk.

"Just take her off for a minute," Frank said, smiling, "so we can get some good shots."

"She's *nursing.*"

"She's asleep," Frank pointed out.

"If you have to take pictures," I said, "go ahead. But diffuse the flash so you don't hurt her eyes."

Frank moved in close and started clicking. He pulled the receiving blanket aside so Carolina's body was exposed. I pulled it back over her.

At two o'clock, after Mark and Ruby left, we went to bed. I wanted Carolina to sleep with us, but Frank was worried he'd crush her, so she slept in a cedar cradle beside me. I was up twice during the night to feed her. Back with Frank, I wanted to be held, but he groaned and turned sleepily away when I touched him.

In the morning, none too impressed, he showed me the fingerprint bruises I'd left on his arms during labour.

A few days later, I was bending over Carolina on the bed. She was wearing blue terry sleepers with snaps up their front and down their legs. She was lying on white chenille. Her blue eyes—that dark and nearly foggy blue of birth—were open and she was staring at me. I had just had her at my breast; she had eaten stomachfuls, the tiny glutton. I looked down at her looking up at me. I began to feel dizzy with love. This was my daughter, my Carolina, a person who was now all to me in the world. I felt as if we shared skin and hearts, as indeed, just days before, we had, when she was me and I was her, indivisible.

If I ever believed in God, this was the moment. Carolina struck divinity into my heart.

I was a mother. For the first few days I wandered the streets with Carolina strapped to my stomach, her lovely head cradled at my shoulder. We went out in the morning and again in the afternoon and at twilight. I hadn't anything else to do but care for Carolina and meander. I noticed rain and sun and the curious shapes of clouds in the sky. I especially noticed the colour of light. Several times I drove Carolina to a nearby lake to sit on the empty dock. Once, by the shore, I'd dangled her feet, but the water—its coldness, the surprise of it—had frightened her. Her cries caused my milk to let down, great squirt guns of milk that dripped down my belly and soaked the waistband of my pants. But I was captivated. I memorized her over and over; every day she was brand new, with a new repertoire of facial expressions, new sounds to her cries, new ways to kick her legs. I'd have been happy to stop time any one of those days. It wouldn't have mattered. A spool of one looping day, again and again.

3

OF COURSE I had to leave Carolina, though. Midway through her first week I went out without her. Frank was home. Jumpily, my breasts sore with milk, I went to town to shop.

I rushed home and through the back door, settling the groceries on the kitchen table. The house smelled faintly of ammonia. In the living room, Carolina was asleep on Frank's shoulder, in her blue sleepers. My milk let down. Frank didn't notice me—his eyes were shut—so I tiptoed closer, my heart filling. We really *were* a family.

The couch blocked my view. Carolina was nestled into Frank's neck. When she woke her cheeks would show the pattern of terrycloth; Frank was wearing the navy robe I'd given him for Christmas.

But then, as I crept forward, I noticed Frank was busy in his lap, not asleep as I'd first figured. What he was busy with didn't register for a minute. I only took in the scene—the room, Carolina, the open robe, the moving hand—and refused to bring thought to it. My mouth was open to say hello; I closed it. I reopened it. I closed it again. Frank was masturbating. Frank, holding Carolina, was near to orgasm.

I was rooted to the spot. I watched Frank come, gobs of semen shooting to the legs of Carolina's sleepers. It was that sight, the sight of Frank ejaculating on Carolina, that got me moving.

I wrenched Carolina from Frank's shoulder. Shocked awake, she let go with screams.

"How *dare* you!" I yelled above her wails.

Frank came to in slow motion. His penis was still weakly spurting. His eyes rolled up and settled on mine.

Holding Carolina, I had my hands in his cum. It was hot and sticky. I jiggled the baby, working automatically to soothe her, but my movements were too sharp and she only screamed louder.

Frank wasn't reacting.

"How *dare* you masturbate?" I shouted. "How *could* you, Frank?" I jostled Carolina in arcs, back and forth and up and down.

Frank reached for a box of tissues on the side table, pulled one out and swiped at himself. Finally he closed his robe.

"Frank, answer me, goddamn it. How could you?"

But Frank just stared up at me, his blue eyes devoid of fear or guilt or surprise.

I laid the shrieking Carolina on the couch and grabbed Frank by the shoulders, shaking him hard. "Tell me. Tell me what the goddamned hell you think you're doing!" Suddenly I was crying, the tears flying off my face. "Get out! Get the hell away from my baby." I pushed him, then spat in his face.

I snatched Carolina up and ran to her room. Repulsed, I stripped off her blue sleepers. I'd been meaning to save them because they were her first clothes, but now I held them with the tip of my index finger and thumb and dropped them into the garbage. Carolina looked blurry through my tears. I changed her diaper and dressed her again and sat in the rocker to nurse her. At last my anger receded and my tears subsided. I sang Carolina a nursery rhyme, my voice flat. When she finished at my left breast, I moved her to my right. When she went to sleep I laid her in her crib and wound her mobile. Then I tied up the garbage bag.

I heard Frank in the shower. Moving mechanically, I started water for coffee, did the dishes and swept the floor. Frank didn't look at me as he passed wrapped in a towel, but when he reappeared dressed, he stood in the doorway repeating my name.

I ignored him. I poured myself a coffee and sat at the table with the newspaper.

"Look," Frank said. "It didn't mean anything."

I pulled the front section free.

"Men just get erections, Ellen," he said. "We don't have control over it. It was a coincidence I was holding Carolina. I walked her around because she was crying and when she fell asleep I sat down. I didn't want to put her in her crib in case I woke her up. And then I was thinking of you, Ellen. I was thinking of how pretty you are." He shrugged. "I got horny."

I didn't acknowledge him.

"We haven't had sex in weeks, Ellen."

I looked at him hard. "You want me to have sex?" I asked disbelievingly. "With stitches?"

"No, no, it's not that, honey. It's just... I miss you."

"That's irrelevant. You just masturbated holding our daughter."

"I told you," he said, "that just happens. I get erections all the time. All men do."

I looked at him skeptically.

"Erections, Ellen, they don't mean anything. You're right to be upset—I know what it must have looked like—but erections are a dime a dozen. It had absolutely nothing to do with Carolina. Please, honey, please believe me."

"I want you to tell me something, Frank," I said. "With complete honesty. Are you sexually"—I searched for the word—"*aroused* by Carolina?"

"I swear to you, Ellen, the baby never crossed my mind." Tears were welling in his eyes. He sagged into a chair across from me. "I couldn't stand to lose you, Ellen. You—you and Carolina—you're my girls. You're my whole life. I love you."

"Bastard," I said, but without much feeling.

"I only wanted you so bad that before I knew what I was doing, I was doing it."

I nodded reluctantly. It was possible, even probable. "I'm sorry I spat on you."

"No," Frank said, "*I'm* sorry. I'm the one who should be apologizing. Forgive me?"

I nodded.

"Forgive me really?"

"Really," I said. "I really do."

≈

1959

I have a sparrow baby I've been feeding with an eyedropper. Most every bird we kids bring home dies, but my sparrow, Sylvia, is actually growing. I am her mommy.

Until my father—oops, an accident! so sorry, Ellen—rolls the tack house door right over her and squashes her dead.

I have mouse babies, seven naked pink mice I feed with an eyedropper. There are always animals around, dogs and cats and horses, a stray goat and an eagle and an owl and bunnies and raccoons we domesticate and garter snakes, and now my mouse babies.

Till Dad buries six of them alive when one dies.

Daddy catches a rabbit in the forest where he keeps traps. Where's my brother, Laurence? He should be here. Poor little Bunny isn't moving. Daddy carries the bunny by her back legs and she's limp and we're beside the eagle's cage and Daddy throws Bunny on the ground. Daddy takes out his pocketknife and flips it open, hard shiny silver, and as I bend to see if I can make Bunny better, Daddy plunges his knife into her tummy and takes her skin off.

≈

I was not long in my idyll with Carolina. Life was messy and demanding. There were a thousand chores. Each needed to be done either with an infant in my arms—a fruitless pursuit—or while Carolina slept. I took to using her down time to catch up on housework; while she slept I baked or scrubbed. I gulped my food while she nursed; everything was done on the run. Hours were sucked away and I ran, I ran, I picked up my legs and ran, satisfaction out of sight, hoping only to keep the worst at bay. Frank complained bitterly. He said I had eyes only for Carolina. He said he'd appreciate it if I'd at least keep the place picked up and get to the laundromat twice a week.

Frank, if he felt like it, went out without a thought for Carolina. When I went out, I took Carolina, satchels of supplies and elaborate plans. I resented Frank's freedom. What was it like to assume Carolina was cared for? To say, I'm going to the bar, catch you later?

But I did love being with my daughter. I laid her in my lap and played games with her feet and toes, snarfling them with my mouth, playing pattycake, always watching her eyes to check if I was pleasing her. I coaxed her first smiles, her first giggles. I carried her everywhere, showing her the world. Here is a caterpillar, Carolina, I'd say as she obliviously slumbered, and caterpillars make cocoons, then break free as butterflies. Here is a bubble, Carolina, see it catch the light and make a rainbow, see how it floats and pops.

I didn't even mind the night feedings. Waking to her cries was rough, but once we were settled in the rocker and she was suckling, I took time to notice the stillness of night. These were our most intimate moments. Here it was only Carolina and me.

In June, Carolina became colicky. This was a different potato. She screamed endlessly. I knew she was in pain; her tummy was hard and her cries were bitter. The doctor recommended Gripe Water and spaced feedings but Carolina was used to eating on demand, used to having her hunger instantly appeased; now she screamed at being denied. There were days when I nearly threw her at Frank when he came in from work, days I walked her and walked her till my feet were sore, days she howled from dawn till dusk and most of the night. When she slept I was alarmed by silence, the sound of no sound. I tiptoed.

If the phone or a knock on the door disturbed her, I burst into tears.

Sometimes Frank woke Carolina through some carelessness, and I turned on him viciously. He didn't care the way a mother cared, I thought. He went through the motions, that's all, walking or bathing Carolina, but he didn't—couldn't—care enough to please me.

Frank's brother Dennis needed a place to stay. He moved his things into our basement, where he spent long hours painting. Sometimes he'd climb the stairs and spell me, watching Carolina so I could get something else done.

It was a warm summer. Carolina was so often feeding that I didn't always bother to button my shirt. My breasts weren't sexual; they were refillable bottles Carolina drained on her new schedule, twelve times a day.

Late one afternoon Frank grabbed me and yanked me into a corner of the kitchen. Dennis had Carolina in her bedroom, changing her; I was about to feed her. My shirt was open.

"Ellen, Christ, I'm sick of this."

"Let go of my arm."

"That's my brother in there, for God's sake. You're behaving like a slut." Frank's eyes bugged out. "You walk around here like Dennis isn't a man, like he has no sexual feelings."

"Lay off, Frank. You're hurting me."

"Just do up your shirt. If you aren't nursing Carolina, I mean it, keep it closed."

"Are you threatening me?"

"Just do it." Frank threw my arm down and stomped away.

≈

1965

Dad has been gone almost two years. I'm glad. We all are. It scares me to see him. I like it, sort of, because he buys me lime sherbet, but Dad is scary.

All the relatives say Mom did it. Mom drove Dad away because she's crazy. My grandparents, her mother and father, say Mom is crazy.

Mom buys us ducks—a duckload, she calls them, twenty-four yellow chirpers we put under incubating lights. When they grow Mom fills a wading pool with water and has us kids upend crates for steps. The ducks dive and pop up. Mom takes pictures.

My father hit my mother. I watched him. That's what no one ever guessed.

≈

By mid-July Carolina's colic became episodic. I, who had thought to live with an inconsolable daughter forever, felt free to get a job. I hadn't been comfortable unemployed. I'd been trained in psychology; now I wanted to work in my field. I found a job in a treatment centre for autistic children. If there was one thing I liked better than kids, it was weird kids. I could help them. I could reach them. I was good at it.

Dennis agreed to babysit in exchange for room and board. I worked strange hours, evenings and sometimes overnights, and more than full-time. I loved how newly competent I felt away from Carolina's colic and Frank's grumpiness, how good it was to have my own substantial pay cheque.

Now I barely saw Frank. His schedule was a strict daytime one, training horses and teaching riding. We hadn't ever talked much; now we never did. In bed, the times we found ourselves together there, we turned our backs to each other, bedside lights on, reading through a stubborn, growing tension.

He wanted me to quit my job. I refused. "I don't see why you can't stay home with her," he said again and again. Neither did I, but I couldn't. I supposed I was a bad mother and probably—my secret worry—crazy. Because wasn't it insane the way I didn't want to be home full-time with my daughter? Wasn't it crazy that every time I looked at Frank, instead of feeling love I felt revulsion?

Carolina grew. Before I realized it she was sitting up, cutting teeth, crawling, then walking. Before I knew it she was off my breast—a relief to Frank, though a loss to me—and eating solid food. Carolina, with wispy curls of black hair spilling down her back, with a pointing finger asking, "What dat?" and "Why? Why? Why?" I was her encyclopedia, the agent of her discoveries.

As for Frank, things between us kept deteriorating. Some days it seemed that all we did was curtly pass Carolina back and forth. We'd come to some impasse, some divide, and the distance we kept between us was cavernous. Blaming myself—probably my stubbornness about working or my reluctance to have sex had caused it—changed nothing. I couldn't stand Frank Moore. It didn't matter whether I was crazy, I couldn't bear to be around him. I thought of winter, summer, winter, years tumbling over themselves.

When Carolina turned a year old, I decided to leave Frank and move to a small town on Vancouver Island. It felt like someone else had control of me. Such was my guilt at leaving Frank, a certainly upstanding man, and at removing his daughter from him, that I couldn't acknowledge the decision as my own. Rather I thought I was being "compelled." I "had to" go. When Frank asked me why, I shrugged my shoulders.

"I don't know," I said, swallowing fear.

"You don't know?"

I shrugged again.

He smiled enigmatically and said he'd help me pack.

"You'll *help* me?" I squeaked.

"I'll take a truck load over for you."

"Oh," I said, scrutinizing him. But if he had a reaction to my news, it wasn't visible.

Frank might have been distant and closed to me, but he wasn't to Carolina; the older she grew, the more he enjoyed spending time with her. Nevertheless, I felt I'd die if I stayed with him. When I thought of staying, my eyes crowded with unbidden memories of my father, and then Frank, too, seemed dangerous.

Insanity ticked in the dark, hidden inside. My feelings were strong; they bristled up from the deep and stood on my skin, obvious to everyone. They left stains, on me and on Frank. That was what Frank implied, what Frank's father said, what my sister said, what even my friend Ruby said. I didn't run from Frank, they said to me, but from myself.

I didn't have a job in the new town I'd moved to, and when my money ran out I applied for welfare. I had always been frightened of people in authority; this was, so far, my worst encounter with them. My worker was a woman and she was nice enough to me, but I hung my head.

Yet I felt sane in my squatty apartment near the sea with Carolina. Sometimes I was overwhelmed at so *much* time parenting—I knew no one and had no income to buy breaks—but overall, I was content. Carolina and I could do free things, go to parks and for walks, and I was continually fascinated by her development. She was fun. I missed working a lot, but I wasn't sure I should look for a job, since that would mean leaving my daughter in daycare.

Carolina had a pink security blanket. It was one of the receiving blankets I'd covered her with early in life; by the end of her colic bout it was attached to her like hair or a leg. We called this dingy thing Blankie. Blankie was a first-line defence, a habit, an irritatingly human bit of cloth. Whenever Carolina was fed up, Blankie went over her head. Whenever Carolina had a bath, Blankie sat on the toilet seat watching. Whenever I washed Blankie, Carolina wailed. Often Blankie spoke, giving Carolina dialogue: "Blankie says I don't *like* peas, Mommy."

Frank was in and out, staying with us frequently on weekends. That was okay. I liked him much better again now that I didn't have to live with him. Eventually, after I'd been gone nearly a year, he convinced me to move back to Vancouver. I agreed, with one proviso: we wouldn't cohabit. I knew—or assumed, I guess, because he never said—that he thought I was pigheaded. But I was firm: I wouldn't live with him. It was a moot point at first, because for our first two months back, Frank was away up north.

One afternoon, shortly after Frank's return, Carolina said, "I used to have a different daddy."

I was buttering bread at our kitchen counter. I turned and looked at my daughter. A little more than two years old, she was working on a puzzle of the Old Woman Who Lived in a Shoe. Carolina loved puzzles and went through as many as I could provide. I haunted a teachers' supply store, but even those expensive stocks were exhaustible. I'd taken to putting groups of ten puzzles on high cupboard shelves, then, when Carolina grew bored, exchanging them for her current ones. It sort of worked, except Carolina's mind was agile—she hadn't lost her facility with the old ones. She was like that with everything, hauntingly precocious. Her vocabulary, for instance, was vast, even if her enunciation was typically muddled.

Frank lived around the corner from us in a bachelor apartment. He'd just the day before returned Carolina from a week's vacation.

"What do you mean, honey?" I said. Frank had driven her up the Sunshine Coast; they'd stayed with my brother, Laurence, who'd moved there a year earlier, and then gone camping.

She creased her forehead, a piece of puzzle clamped in her plump fingers. Her blue eyes contrasted with her dark hair. She repeated it with a little more emphasis. "I used to have a *different* daddy."

I put down the knife and knelt beside her chair. "Pumpkin?" I said. A different father? Did she mean she'd forgotten him before their trip, when Frank hadn't seen her for nearly two months? "You just have one daddy, Carolina. Only one."

Her puzzle pieces had little wooden pegs for her pudgy fingers. She manoeuvred the piece she was holding onto the board. "I had a different daddy," she said stubbornly.

"Sugar, you didn't. Honestly."

But Carolina peered out the window, ignoring me. There was a wedding at the church across the street; we'd been waiting to see the bride and groom.

I hauled out our photo albums. "But pumpkin, see here? Here's Daddy holding you just after you were born. And here he is again, a picture from just last week, from your vacation."

Carolina watched with a furrowed brow. She paid attention to the pictures all right, but when I closed the cover she turned back to her puzzle. Now she seemed uncertain, a little afraid.

"Do you mean Daddy with a beard? Or Daddy with a moustache? That Daddy *looks* different?" Lately Frank had been growing facial hair.

She shook her head and protruded her lower lip. Her eyes were full of mistrust. "He looks the same, Mommy. But he used to be different."

"How was he different, Carolina?"

Now her lip trembled and tears spilled onto her cheeks. "I don't like you," she whined. Her eyes were cloudy. She pulled Blankie over her head. "You're a bad mommy, Mommy."

I went back to making sandwiches. Whatever she was saying, whatever she meant—most likely, I concluded, she'd forgotten Frank—was not about to come clear. "You want peanut butter and jam, buttercup? Or a hug, maybe?"

"Mom?" she said, her voice muffled by the blanket.

"Uh-huh?"

"Just peanut butter."

Over the summer I began to notice unsettling changes in Carolina; she seemed edgy and fearful. Sometimes I attributed behaviours like bed wetting or nightmares or tantrums in public to the insecurity of our move or to spending nights away from me when she was with Frank—she was so little to be deprived of her mother, even just overnight—and sometimes, when I could uncover no explanation, I blamed myself. Her behaviour changes were surely caused by my inadequate parenting. If I were more patient … more even-handed… I blamed myself even as Carolina grew worse.

She was frightened to sleep. Reluctant to walk. Ghosts took up residence in our toilet, amorphous, squashy grey ghosts she'd have to sit over if she graduated from her potty seat. Daddy, she said, had witches in him. She herself had "blood-aches," whatever those were, and painful, foul-smelling genital rashes that I showed her how to dab with Penaten cream and that the doctor ascribed to the use of bubble bath, though they didn't subside when I stopped using it. She often wet her bed. When I asked her what kind of cereal she wanted for breakfast, she sometimes replied with baby talk: "Goo ga pease, Mommy."

I was confused; I couldn't say what was wrong. I felt I should be able to explain: Yes, 10 per cent the move, 30 per cent missing her father, 20 per cent a combination of babysitters she didn't like and visitors; 10 per cent potty training, and 30 per cent me, somehow me. But I could not. Instead I did as any mother would. I tried to ease Carolina's burdens. Even if I could not understand, I could do a better job of parenting her.

I would lie with her when she needed to sleep, read her a story, then hold her in my arms while she drifted off. I loved the fruity, coconuty smell of her. I loved putting my face to her hair and breathing in. I'd stroke her hair from her face or skirt a soft finger over her back, drawing endless circles. Even so, she'd report nightmares when she woke, her big eyes wide with fear. She couldn't describe the dreams, though, just shook her head and reached for her Speak & Spell. "Spell fox," the machine intoned.

Carolina pushed F. "Mom, what's next?"

"O, honey."

"Next?"

"The letter X."

The machine said, "That is correct. Now spell dog."

"D-o-g. Right, Mom?"

"Right."

I was shooting out sparks of questions to Frank and friends: What? Why? They too suggested our move, the separation. They suggested the terrible twos. Then quietly, concern rimming their voices, they suggested I was making a big deal out of nothing.

It was difficult to spend my days with Carolina and believe I was overreacting. I was her mother. If I was noticing a clear change, if what I was noticing was disturbing, if Carolina was troubled, which she seemed obviously, weirdly to be, then there had to be a culprit. And quite possibly it was me.

I wanted to say, No, I have done thus and so to nurture my child. No, I have never hit her. No, I have never spoken sharply. But there were times I was firmly sick of her presence, days I resented doing for her, days I banished her to her room only because I was desperate to have ten minutes unbroken by her chatter, when I thought I would explode if she asked me one more question: Why do magnets work, Mommy? Can I have an elephant? Why do brides wear white? Why is there sand on a beach, Mommy? Where does air come from? If I was a fish, Mommy, would you still be my mommy? If I was a tiger I would probably eat you up, Mommy, 'cause that's what tigers do; is that okay, Mommy? How come flowers grow? Mommy, when I grow up to be big, will I be your mommy and you be my little girl? Can I have ice cream? How come I don't go to school? What's a rhinoceros look like, Mommy? Knock-knock. Who's there? It's me, it's Carolina!

I did raise my voice. I was perhaps too strict about her picking up her toys, using the words please and thank you, too eager to civilize her so I'd be seen as a good mother. Finger-paints only in the bathroom. Plastic under the table when she used poster paints. And over and over, the dictum to avoid throwing balls in the house.

One day, after I'd said it for the third time, when she knew I meant business, Carolina threw five balls out the window.

It was rough and chancy being a single mother. I often imagined it as a state of siege, mothers in apartments and houses all around the world, behind sandbags, praying for reinforcements. The children were the reason: extravagant, cocksure and demanding, the children had us by the hearts and throats. Love pummelled us.

We mothers needed each other. Childless friends acted as though I'd been rendered witless by procreation. In their presence I tried to remember to speak of things other than Carolina, but Carolina was my spark, my fire. Knee-high to a grasshopper, she was a flashlight that exposed my skies and swamps, the extremes I hadn't known I possessed. The only people who understood this were other mothers. We sought each other out. We put our children in junior gymnastics and sat on the sidelines chatting. We pushed our kids on swings and talked. We joined mothering groups and spilled our woes.

My closest friends were Teresa, single mom of three-year-old Samantha, Leslie, single mom of two-year-old Sky, and Jean. Certainly I had other friends—Frank's brother Dennis and his new wife Eleanor, my brother Laurence, Ruby in a lackadaisical way—and acquaintances and old work buddies, but these, Teresa and Leslie and Jean, had depth, detail and colour.

≈

1962

Very late one night, Mom scoops me from bed. I haven't wet, yet, so my nightgown is dry. Mom whispers that Belinda, our mare, is foaling. "I want you to see it," she says. There've been weeks and weeks of waiting—Mom in the kitchen with the scratchy intercom linked to the barn, all that neighing. Mom says that horses sound different when they're about to have babies, that she'll recognize the sounds. Even so, she pops out to the barn, usually my father's place (since he's the horse fancier, the one who builds up the hobby farm of hunters and jumpers), several times a day.

Mom leaves the other kids asleep and carries me like an infant in her arms, down the stairs and out the back door. It's cool and wet. As she carries me down the path past the paddock and outbuildings, I look straight up at the stars.

Dad's already in the barn. Belinda's in the fifth stall under hot yellow incubating lights, whinnying and trying to dodge the pain. Mom props me on fresh straw. The pregnant mare's eyes are round—the whites show. Mom's soft voice settles her some. Finally Belinda crumples to her knees, big horse falling, and rolls onto her side.

I stare hard as the baby comes out of her. There've been other babies born dead, babies Dad's buried in the barnyard, but I'm not scared. Dad holds the mare's tail out of the way. The little foal comes out not moving. Mom, cooing reassurances by Belinda's head, moves aside as the mare jerks, then curls around to lick her baby. She has a big pink tongue. I can see the baby's sac lift off, stretch and finally break.

"It's a filly," Dad says grumpily.

Mom and I don't care. Mom pulls me onto her lap. Just as soon as Belinda has the sac free and the afterbirth eaten, she heaves back up. The filly, shaking wildly, tries to get up too. Her legs are like sticks and don't hold her; she struggles straight on one leg, then folds back down. Or Belinda pushes her back down, licking her. She has very black, wet hair and large soft eyes.

Mom wraps her arms around me tight.

At last the filly stands. Immediately she noses under her mom and butts, looking for milk.

Mom says, "What shall we call her? Ellen?"

"Louise," I say. "Her name is Louise."

"Louise," Mom repeats, smiling as if I'm funny. "Louise it is."

≈

4

I WAS SLEEPING with Frank again by midsummer. Sex was like a suitcase I couldn't get closed. I bulged shirt sleeves and pant legs. I bulged the memory of sensations. Finally I was full up and wild to have sex, to have even Frank.

We had sex covertly, behind closed doors, under covers, secreted in the depths of night while Carolina slumbered.

I seemed never to have left him.

In the kitchen one late August morning, while I sat at the table reading as Carolina ate her Cheerios, I felt a strange stirring in my uterus. Generally I felt nothing from my uterus; period cramps were abdominal and so diffused they mostly hurt my back. This, however, was specific, far inside, in just one small area. I pushed back my chair, undid my zipper and settled my hands on my skin. I could feel a slight vibration. Inside my womb, I felt something like an adrenalin rush. It was vaudevillian, I thought, sitting there: brash, centre-stage stuff.

Then a thought came to me, an exuberant, firecracking thought, and I realized exactly what it must be: conception. A fertilized egg implanting in my uterine wall.

I was pregnant again.

As it turned out, so was Teresa, who'd seduced a twenty-six-year-old virgin she had no intention of living with. And so was Jean.

Oh, the torpor. This pregnancy, this child unknown in my womb, implanted like a lottery win. This child I believed was a boy, who grew in testosterone bursts, so that at a month along I showed and had gained fifteen pounds.

Frank said, "Have you considered abortion?"

Frank saw the baby's advent as a sort of sexual penalty: he wanted it scraped and flushed from my womb. And though I thought abortion an undeniable right, I could not rid myself of *this* child, this snappy baby who'd come in with a kick.

I told Frank no.

What bravado. I was pregnant with a second child. I was shaky, there in my tiny apartment with Carolina. I had this single, firm spot: I would not abort.

When Frank asked me to come back—he actually said *home*: "Ellen, come home"—I barely blinked.

After we'd found a house together, I returned to work in an effort to feel better about myself. I wasn't otherwise competent: if I were, Carolina would be ordinary. And Carolina wasn't ordinary any more—she was neurotic. I found a job working with autistic adults. I worked a shift that began just before Frank got home so I needed a sitter for only an hour. Away from Frank and from Carolina's demands, work felt like a vacation. My clients were often violent, though. By the time I left that job, when I was eight and a half months pregnant, I'd had a broken nose and a punched belly.

Being at home often felt like walking through jelly, like trying to sculpt with air. Work had been clear-cut.

It was hard to ascertain what Carolina, now three, understood about birth. She knew she would have a new sister or brother—a sister, she adamantly told me—but past that? How to explain home birth? My midwife loaned me a book that had an illustration of a woman receiving an internal examination, a mother working hard during labour and, on the last page, a gushy baby appearing.

Carolina wanted to see the internal again. We were snuggled up beside each other in her room in our new house. I showed her the illustration and explained that when mommies were growing babies, doctors or midwives examined them to make sure the babies were healthy.

"Look, Mommy!" Carolina said, raising her legs so her nightie slid up. "I can do it too!" She pushed a finger out of sight.

"No," I said faintly, pushing down her legs, "Carolina, that's just for grownups."

"I can do it to you," Carolina said. "I can be your midwife, Mommy, I can."

The book slipped to the floor. I wondered how Carolina knew where her vagina was in the first place. "Honey, sweetheart, you can feel the baby right here." I pulled one of her hands to my pregnant middle. "Feel it? The baby's kicking again."

"No, Mommy," Carolina said, pulling free. "I *know* how to do it."

"Look, Carolina, it's not okay for children to do that. Only grownups can, doctors who use special gloves."

"I can use my mittens," Carolina said.

"No, Carolina." But she was up off the bed and gone. I tried to pick up the book, but I couldn't get my hands to work. Usually I was hot as a furnace; now I shivered. This book, I thought, kicking it with my toe, was her introduction to the birds and bees. So how come she knew so much?

Carolina flew back in. Her hands were proudly held up; covering them were Baggies, lunch Baggies for Frank's sandwiches.

"Frank," I said later when Carolina was asleep, "I need to talk to you." I explained what had happened.

Frank thought my concerns were silly.

"You're right," I agreed finally. "I know you're right." Then a thought struck me. "But why doesn't she have a hymen?"

Frank shook his head impatiently. He raked his fingers through his hair.

"Well, Frank, she doesn't. I saw her finger go inside."

"Ellen, drop it. You always do this. You always make mountains out of molehills."

"Maybe it is a mountain."

"We take Carolina horseback riding," Frank pointed out.

I thought about that, how riding purportedly broke hymens. Probably riding had broken mine—I hadn't seemed to have one. I slouched down in my chair, petulant. "I'm tired of being pregnant, Frank. You know what I wish? I wish I didn't even have to go into labour. I wish I could just wake up and there'd be a baby here." In my belly the baby was kicking up a storm, strongly enough to hurt me.

Frank clicked on a baseball game.

It was 11:30 on a Tuesday night in June. I had spent the day at Jericho Beach with Teresa and Leslie. In my eighth month of pregnancy, Leslie had moved to Nelson in the province's interior, but she'd returned for the birth, staying across town at her sister's place. It was cool for June, only washily sunny; we'd all worn sweaters or windbreakers. Carolina and Sky and Sammy, fast friends, dug in the sand.

I was grumpy. The baby had been doing jumping jacks in my belly almost as if punching its way out. I'd been short with Carolina and snarly with Frank. I hurt. At ten that night, after Frank had gone to bed, I'd had a bath, hoping the heat would put the baby to sleep; when that failed, I'd lain down still being hit. That was when the bomb exploded: labour, sudden and huge.

There was an inbreath, slow, sucking into me like a wave as it tunnelled sand. Outbreath a hiss, a snake uncoiling. Another surge and inbreath slow.

Frank jerked awake, groaning. I couldn't tell him I was in labour—there was too much pain to speak. "Jesus Christ, Ellen," he mumbled, "not tonight." But he rolled from bed. I tried to set up the camera for Leslie to take pictures, but after I got the film loaded, I dropped the camera. I was dizzy and shaking violently.

Inbreath. Hard. Outbreath. Hard like glass shards.

Inbreath. No time between contractions. I stumbled into the living room. Frank was talking on the phone, calling our supporters.

Outbreath. Through clenched teeth I blurted to Frank, "Tell them maybe, I'm not sure."

Frank, though, was certain. My helpers were certain, too, hearing my breath—so loud, so definite—over the phone.

I felt so far away. Time telescoped. I circled warily, watching and stumbling. Frank carried the baby's bassinet out of our bedroom.

When my midwife, Julie, arrived, she smiled and hugged me. She pulled me into the bedroom and checked me. I was already seven centimetres dilated, in heavy labour.

Somehow I made it to Carolina's room. "Love," I said, gently shaking her shoulder, "Mommy's having the baby now. Do you want to get up?"

Carolina came instantly awake. She threw her arms around my neck. "Pumpkin," I said, "I can't carry you. You have to walk."

"Mom?" she said. "Is Sammy here?"

"Yup," I said, forcing back squeals of pain.

The house bulged with people. Teresa, pregnant, and Samantha. Leslie, her arms full of flowers, and her two-year-old son. My pregnant friend Jean. Frank and Julie. Soon toys were scattered everywhere, making my travel around the living room an obstacle course.

I began, without inhibition, to make more noise. Inbreath, forceful, vacuuming air to fill me. Outbreath and I screamed, or sang or moaned or chanted.

Julie and Jean ripped open sterile packages of sheets, clothing and supplies. Frank boiled water. Leslie tended the kids.

Teresa walked behind me, braiding my hair. She fanned my sweaty body and rubbed my shoulders.

I hewed rough circles. Inbreath. I was astonished at the amount of air I pulled into my lungs. My outbreath with its noise released and steadied me, let go the blasting pain. During every break I negatively anticipated the next contraction.

Teresa still moved behind me. She joked about the house tilting when I stumbled. Sweat dripped. The house was hot, hot, hot. The kids kept laughing. I felt a downward spiral.

There was blood on my thighs. My mucus plug had broken.

Julie guided me to bed. In navy corduroys and a soft Indian print shirt, she bent to take the fetal heart tones.

Carolina offered raspberry tea popsicles she'd already sucked. I slurped at them, relieved to wet my parched throat. Teresa pressed a compress to my forehead.

During another vaginal exam, Julie said the sac holding my waters was bulging; I had to stay put until it broke. I couldn't say how much I wanted to get up.

The waters sprayed six feet and coated the wall across the room. I watched the spreading stain on the peach wall.

"Time?" someone asked. It was one o'clock, only one and a half hours since I began labour.

The little ones climbed onto the bed beside me. Leslie took pictures.

Julie said not all of my cervix was dilated. She pushed it away from the baby's head; Teresa soothed me as I screamed and jerked back. I pleaded for Julie to stop, stop the exam, make the urge to push go away. Inbreath. Outbreath, sobbing.

"Okay, now push, Ellen," I finally heard. "Give it your all."

Inbreath, then push. There was no bigger need. Teresa said I was pulling up instead of pushing down. I concentrated, forcing my body and brain to remember pushing Carolina out.

Julie announced that she could see the baby's head in the birth canal. She sounded elated, rapt.

"What?" I gasped.

"I can see the baby's head," she repeated. "You're doing fine. A few more of those pushes and it'll be out."

"Out?" I yelled, surprised. "Out of my body?" I pushed and grunted.

"Okay," said Teresa, "now pant." She leaned in close, right over my face, and showed me how. But I was pushing. I couldn't pant and push at the same time. Teresa was an orchestra in my face, hot breath and sensible, intelligent love. I pushed hugely.

One moment the baby was beginning to crown, the next I saw a spidery monkey, all limbs and blue-red wet tiny naked wrinkles in Julie's arms, flying to my belly. A shout. "2:19!"

Born. From somewhere appeared a blanket to cover it. Julie suctioned briefly. There was a plaintive wail as air was sucked into new, untried lungs, and then quiet breath, alert eyes, a puzzled interest. I clung to this tiny, astonishing bundle.

Julie caught her breath. "She's beautiful."

"She?" I watched the cord stretched to my child pulsing.

Teresa confirmed it. "You have a daughter."

Julie, Teresa, Leslie and the children all sang praises to the baby's beauty and health. She began to suckle eagerly at my breast. She had a lot of hair and a red, flat-nosed face. She was ugly. She murmured and cooed.

Beside me Carolina said, "I *told* you it was a girl."

"You were right," I said, holding out my hand. "You have a new baby sister."

"Amy," Carolina said, remembering the name Frank and I had chosen for a girl.

"Amy," I agreed, shaky and weak, pulling Carolina close. She leaned into me.

We stayed like that for a long time. Julie needed to stitch me. Then Teresa brought in strawberries and champagne.

When Amy was an hour and a half old, I carried her to the living room for Carolina to hold. I arranged Carolina in a chair with a pillow in her lap and pillows on either side. "C'mon," she said, "c'mon, Mommy," and wiggled her fingers. Her grin was enormous. Carefully I lowered Amy, who shocked at the loose, airborne ride into Carolina's arms.

Carolina's eyes widened in their sockets. She was stopped like that for a second, her mouth fully open. Then she cried, "Mommy, it's heavy!" and dropped Amy fast.

Amy was a dulcet infant. In bed with me—we slept together while Frank used a foamy in Carolina's room—she cooed and snuffled and sighed her pleasure. I hardly lost sleep; when she was hungry she babbled a sound like "mum, mum, mum" till I woke and fed her, still lying in bed. Her first weeks were a confection, a delectation. On her second day, latching her dizzy vision to my face, she smiled. In her hushed infant brain were the beginnings of patterns, imprints of sight and smell, the sound of our house, the feel of diapers strapped across her waist, Carolina's chirruping, Frank's laconic basso, my warm susurrations.

As we'd arranged—I'd convinced him of her special need—Frank took a few days off work to spend with Carolina. While Amy and I woozied through our first week, Frank took Carolina to Stanley Park, the beach, McDonald's. My hope was that Carolina wouldn't feel left out: a mommy who was all hers was gone, transmogrified by this baby Amy into a mommy who didn't get out of bed, a mommy with a baby like a growth at her breast, a mommy who napped afternoons. A mommy for whom the house needed to be quiet.

On her third day, Amy tinged yellow. The sky was sluggish and clouded over. I stood at the window behind lace curtains praying for sun. Otherwise I'd have to admit Amy to a hospital, where, under lights, her jaundice could be cured.

But at noon the clouds parted. I carried Amy and a lawn chair to the sidewalk. For an hour I let the sun's hazy beams caress her newborn skin. When she pinked, the sky closed.

On Amy's fifth night, Teresa's son was born. Amy's first outside trip was to visit Daniel. I was still shaky, still sore with stitches, but I manoeuvred supplies into the car, strapped in Carolina and Amy, and drove across town with welcoming irises. We sent Samantha and Carolina into the yard to play. With Amy, I stretched out on the bed beside Teresa and Daniel. Teresa was beautiful. Daniel was tiny and perfect. I nuzzled Teresa's hair, kissed her cheek and neck.

5

I HAD GOTTEN to the end of my pregnancy and named her Amy, but where to from there? Frank returned to work. I woke and saw diapers, Pablum, highchairs. I could not imagine that Amy would grow, would walk, would attend school. I could not imagine nineteen more years of active motherhood. I was here, grumpily up from bed and holding Amy while I scrambled eggs for Carolina. This goal, each morning this one goal: to get through the day.

I was surprised to discover having two children meant twice the work. Carolina was already—was still—a full-time job. I'd expected Amy would just drip into leftover time. Not Amy, though. Amy was no little trickle. Amy was full-tilt waterfall. Amy was rapids.

"Mommy!" Carolina called. "Amy needs changing, she made a stinky! You better come. Mo-omm, you better hurry, she's pulling her hair."

Any time Amy wound up on her back her little fist slinked up and caught hold of her hair. She looked supremely foolish, no bigger than a minute and with all this long auburn hair spilling out through her clenched fingers. Her averted, berry-red face contorted and she let out rigorous wails of pain. Patiently, Carolina and I undid her fingers, one by one, and lowered her arm.

"Oh, Amy," Carolina said, shaking her head. "Why don't you learn? Why don't you *ever* learn?"

Frank and his goddamn photographs. By the time Amy was a couple of weeks old, he'd gone through about twenty rolls of film. For all that, he'd taken hardly any of Amy and me together. Often I appeared as just a hand in the corner of the frame reaching out to steady her bathinette or hold her hand.

Disturbingly, no pictures of Amy's birth had turned out. Frank had refused to take any and, though Leslie did, I'd forgotten to set the camera's flash so Leslie had gotten duds. Frank actually smiled when I showed him the empty package and blank negatives.

Frank had full-colour close-ups of Amy's drying umbilical stump, pictures of Amy sick with jaundice, pictures of Carolina and Amy nude in the yard, pictures taken at such an angle that the folds of Amy's genitalia focalized. He explained these as art: "The human *form*, Ellen," he said.

One day Amy was a chestnut, glowing and fat, the next she burst. As she grew, I shed her birth mother, chose my footing and stepped back into life. I was tethered to Amy by her bi-hourly need for feedings, but now we had time apart, time Amy slumbered in her bassinet, time I left her entirely either with Teresa, who could nurse her, or with Frank.

It broke her open.

I had been through ordinary baby squalls with Carolina. I had been through colic. But Amy's crying was a new thing altogether. After exhausting Teresa and Jean, who were baffled, and Frank, who purported to be mystified, I explained the symptoms to my doctor.

"She's in a world of her own," I said. "I could hit books together beside her ear and she wouldn't hear it. I call her name or snap my fingers but she's oblivious. Her cries don't sound like hunger or loneliness, they sound like terror." I paused and laughed. "I mean, that sounds ridiculous. What would she be terrified of?"

The doctor examined Amy, who started up crying normally. "Is this what you mean?"

"No," I said. "The other is nothing like this. Her eyes are glazed. She doesn't see anything. I can wave my arms over her face but she doesn't notice."

"I can't find anything wrong physically," the doctor assured me. "Her liver's working. I just don't know, Ellen. I don't know what to tell you."

"You don't think I'm making it up?" I asked, dressing Amy and pulling her close.

"Ellen, the postpartum period is tough. Don't ask so much of yourself. Try to get rest. Try to eat well. Things will calm down."

"But I'm very worried about her," I said.

"Well, certainly, keep an eye on her. But it looks like she's fine. She's healthy. She's putting on weight. She's responsive. I can't say *I* have concerns."

"Thank you," I said. I didn't know whether to be relieved or not. Maybe the doctor was right and I *was* overreacting, blowing Amy's strange crying out of proportion. But then again the spells, which often came on waking, lasted a full twenty or thirty minutes, during which Amy, little nine-pound Amy, shook her head violently and drew her legs up to her tummy and kicked, as if warding something off. Was that it? *Was* Amy warding something off?

Frank called me lazy. In front of company, as if it were a joke, as if it were funny, Frank said, How many mothers does it take to change a light bulb? When the guests gave up he said, One, but she has to get off her ass.

Each week Frank and I split up our discretionary money, usually seventy or eighty dollars. This was the money we had left after bills and grocery shopping. I used mine for the things the kids required during the week, from cotton swabs to diapers to milk. By Wednesday or Thursday I'd be broke. There'd be a new list of things I needed, like batteries for Carolina's Speak & Spell and sour cream, and I'd ask Frank if he had money he could let me have.

"Ellen," he'd say, sighing and reaching into his pocket, pulling out crumpled twenties and tens and fives, "why is it you're broke and I have thirty-seven dollars left?"

I didn't know.

Eventually Frank would pass me a twenty. He'd say, "Make sure it lasts this time."

I'd nod. I'd stand in pharmacies fingering things the girls needed rather than dropping them into the red basket Carolina carried. I'd say, "Well, gals, what do you think? Can we get by without diaper rash cream? Just until Monday?"

Finally I got it. One evening when I was asking for more, I understood that while Frank was only buying beer after work with his money, I was supplying the needs of a family of four with mine.

≈

1964

Mom drives to Niagara Falls. Dad lives near Toronto and we still live in Burlington, but Dad makes her meet him once a month in Niagara Falls, in the parking lot of the Wax Museum.

She tells me to sit still, gets out in the rain and knocks on his car window. Twice, because he pretends not to see her.

When he finally rolls the window down an inch, he passes her a five-dollar bill.

I've heard her beg her parents for money to support us kids. But they side with Dad, believing she is crazy, believing she fooled around on him.

Mom knocks again on Dad's car window. Her hair is starting to look stringy. Drips roll off her nose.

Slowly he rolls the window down. He makes a big show of sliding a couple of twenties off his bankroll. And closes the window again.

Mom sinks to her knees beside Dad's car and bangs her fists on his door. Dad finally tosses the rest of the money out his window and speeds off. Mom crawls after the cash.

I let myself out of the car. I pull Mom's elbow and help her stand up. She looks at me bleakly. "That's it, that's the last straw," she tells me. "I'm divorcing him."

When she shakes her head, big drops of rain land on me.

≈

Laurence and Frank disappeared into our bedroom to watch a ball game. I looked at Brigit, Laurence's girlfriend, and rolled my eyes.

"I'll help you do the dishes," Brigit said. The kids were both asleep. She picked up Frank's plate.

As we cleaned up, I asked Brigit about things with Laurence. My brother was in his late twenties. He'd moved up near Lund on the Sunshine Coast and now he built dulcimers for a living. He'd been dating Brigit for six months.

"He's mad I came down to the city for school," Brigit said. She lifted a plate and dried it. "I don't know if we can keep it going, just weekends, but Laurence wants to try. If you ask me—" Brigit shook her head and grinned.

I thought she meant it was already over with my brother but for the saying so. Brigit was, as Laurence's women always were, beautiful. She was thin and messy with wild sweeps of black hair and high, round, rosy cheeks. She moved languidly. I watched her put dishes on the shelves.

Brigit said, "He's pretty clueless. He'd like me to sit at home, I think, knitting or something."

"Making babies?"

Brigit frowned. "Well, look who's doing the dishes. Not Laurence."

"Not Frank," I added.

"I'd really like to make something of myself. Laurence doesn't see it's not about him. It's something I want for myself."

"I feel drowned no matter what I do," I said, nodding and scrubbing a casserole dish. "If I go back to work, Frank'll be mad because I don't keep up at home. But if I'm home, he calls me lazy."

"He calls you lazy?" Brigit laughed.

"I think he thinks breast-feeding's lazy," I said. "He says, 'Where's my shirt? How come you didn't get the laundry done?'" I paused and rested my wrists against the counter. "You know what he said? I couldn't believe it. He said, 'It's not fair you have breasts, Ellen, and there's nothing I have that I can put in Amy's mouth.'" I made a face, mimicking him.

Brigit laughed. She wiped her hands on her dress and asked if I wanted to have lunch with her sometime.

A month later, when Brigit had broken off with Laurence, she told me she was pregnant. It was Laurence's baby and I felt a sort of proprietary interest.

Jean had had her baby, a big strapping boy she and her partner, Michael, named Bartholomew, or Bart for short. Teresa's son was over a month old already.

"I'm having an abortion," Brigit said.

"Does Laurence know?" I asked.

"Don't tell him. Promise?"

I had Amy on my lap and I bounced her a little too hard. I said, "But he's the father, Brigit."

"He's not involved. It's not Laurence who has to carry it for nine months. Or look after it for twenty years."

I nodded.

"I wondered if you'd come with me," Brigit said. "It's just day surgery. Would you drive me?"

"I don't want you to have an abortion."

Brigit shrugged. The circles of red on her cheeks were vivid.

"But I'll support you," I said and opened my shirt for Amy. "Of course, Brigit. Of course I'll be there."

And I was. Towing two kids, I drove Brigit to the hospital for her abortion.

Brigit and I began spending a lot of time together. Frank noticed a change in me. He started griping about my new friendship, made comments about how I ought to have stuck by Laurence in the breakup, how Brigit was screwed up with what he called "notions," how I ought to be careful.

But I wasn't careful. I adored Brigit's self-realized life. She didn't fall into things the way I seemed to; she made decisions about her life. She was studying creative writing at the university and also taking courses in women's studies. She said things like, "Ellen, do you ever wonder why, when you have twice the education Frank does, you get paid only half the money?" She told me that most single women with kids were poor. That women weren't as crazy as men wanted to think. That rape was legal in marriage, and that there was something called "date rape." That it was impossible for a woman to "ask for it."

I'd talk to Frank about these things later, spurring confusing fights. Under Brigit's influence, the cocoon I was swaddled in was shaking. Frank heard rattles. With each day I spent with Brigit my cocoon grew noisier and more restless.

In mid-July, when Amy was six weeks old, my paid maternity leave ended. I was ambivalent. I wished I could stretch like toffee so I could be in two places at once. I wanted to work—I was committed to returning to the group home and we needed the money—but I hated leaving the kids and finding sitters.

Once, to go to a concert with Frank, I'd left Carolina with a woman who pilfered her security blanket. Frank and I had returned to pick up Carolina. After gathering our daughter and her toys and supplies, I requested her blanket. The woman told me I hadn't brought a blanket. It was pink, I said. No, she said, I saw no such thing. I draped it over that chair back, I said, pointing. No, she said, you did not. I want the blanket, I said. She said, A child that age should be ashamed of needing a security blanket. Give it to me, I said. That's eight dollars, she said. You owe me eight dollars.

I found a woman who lived over a grocery store down the street to look after the girls during the two hours Frank and I were both gone.

But I was antsy. On the hour, I called home from work. After a couple of weeks Frank got ticked off. "What do you think is going to happen while you're gone, Ellen?" he asked me.

"Oh," I said, "well. Nothing. I just feel better if I call."

"Don't call, okay?"

"Frank, I have to call. Let me talk to Carolina."

"She's playing with Oshi from downstairs."

"Can you put Amy up to the phone?"

"Ellen, she's napping."

"How's her rash?"

"Ellen," Frank said. "The girls are fine."

"I left tuna casserole in the fridge." I sighed. "Were things okay at the babysitter's? Have you got enough milk?"

"You left six bottles, Ellen, for heaven's sake. Don't you have work to do?"

"Yeah," I said. "Okay then. I'll call you later. Don't forget to give Carolina her bath. Make sure she brushes her teeth."

"Good-bye, Ellen," Frank said firmly.

"Sure. Okay. Okay. Well, good-bye then."

Inside me it felt like someone was scratching fingernails across a blackboard. Inside it was screechy and sore.

Early in August, I signed Carolina up for Red Cross swimming lessons and Amy for water babies. Twice a week we'd trundle off to the community centre. While I carried Amy into the water, Carolina sat wrapped in a towel by the side of the pool, enjoined to stay still: her lesson followed ours. She pouted and stroked her face with her new yellow blanket, but she didn't move. I and the other mothers ducked and rose, ducked and rose while our babies clutched our necks. Some of the babies wailed, but some of them liked it. Some of them chortled and laughed. Amy usually cried, or looked like she was about to. Babies could swim, the instructor said. Babies naturally knew how. Softly we mothers blew into our babies' faces to cause them to hold their breath, and then dunked. Over and over we dunked. The babies came up with dripping, blinking, astonished faces, sometimes coughing. Then we blew and lowered them away from our bodies so they were swimming face down. We turned them onto their backs as we brought them to the surface. By the end of the classes they were meant to swim solo. They'd hold their breath, roll and surface on their backs and kick to the side of the pool.

It was nerve-wracking.

But within a few weeks Amy was swimming, safely propelling herself to the pool's edge for rescue.

The instructor took underwater photographs. There was three-month-old Amy with her wild auburn hair floating straight up, her lips pursed, her eyes wide as saucers, slicing the waves in her red polka-dot swimsuit.

During Carolina's class—her lessons were in the shallow end and consisted mostly of the kids being coaxed to lower their faces into the water to blow bubbles—Amy and I warmed up in the whirlpool.

≈

1966

My mother lets my little sister and me make her up. We giggle upstairs to her vanity to scoop up cosmetics, then run back to where Mom sits at the kitchen table. I apply rouge and freckles. My sister pulls Mom's hair into pigtails and I help wrap elastics around. Mom looks very young and silly, and my sister and I clap delightedly.

When my mother is good, she is very, very good.

≈

I was at work. It was a Thursday deep into August, just after 7:00 P.M. I called Frank. I wrapped the telephone cord around my fingers and waited.

After twenty rings I gave up. I called Dennis to see if Frank and the girls were at his house. I called Brigit but got no answer. I tapped my fingers on my desk. He had the phone off the hook? Carolina was in the bath and he couldn't leave her? He'd taken the kids to McDonald's?

On my fourth try, long into the series of rings, Frank grabbed up the phone barking, "What?"

In the background my daughters were screaming. "Frank?" I shouted. "What's going on?" I felt instant, runaway fear. I knew those screams. I'd heard those screams from Amy—the terror screams.

"Call back."

"Frank!" I said.

"Not now." Frank slammed down the phone.

Quickly I dialled Teresa.

I heard her gentle hello.

"It's me. Something's wrong. Teresa, I need you to go check what's going on at my place. I called and the girls were screaming blue murder. Frank wouldn't talk to me."

"Honey," she said, "I don't know what you're saying."

"I know it's a lot to ask," I said. "Please, will you go over there?"

"I could call."

"Frank won't answer. He hung up on me. There's some kind of trouble, Teresa."

Teresa was quiet for a moment. Then she said, "Of course I'll go."

"Now?" I said. "Can you go right away? And then call me?"

"Sure," she said reluctantly.

"Don't tell Frank I called you. Please just don't tell Frank, okay? Pretend you're dropping in for a visit. Like you thought I'd be home."

When I got off, I paced. My clients came into the office, in, out; I paced. I picked up the desk clock and shook it. Tick, the second hand said. Tock, the second hand said. Why was I such a long drive away from home?

Finally the phone rang.

"I brought the kids over to see you, Ellen, but when I got here, Frank said you were working. We're just having tea."

"You're at my house?" I said harshly. "Are the girls—"

"Sammy and Carolina are playing in the bedroom. Amy's sound asleep."

"Are you kidding?"

"Frank and Carolina were having rice and veggies."

"Teresa, you should have heard them. I thought . . . " I shook my head. "I thought something big, something major had happened."

"Let's get together for lunch tomorrow. We can take the kids to the park, let Sam and Carolina splash in the wading pool. I'll call you, okay?"

"Teresa?"

"Um?"

"Thanks. I mean it, really. I owe you one."

I fetched a baby bottle from my bag and wandered into the washroom. I sat on the toilet and opened my shirt. My breasts were large and sore. Wincing, I began to massage the right one. My fingers worked out from the base, finding and manipulating my milk ducts. I held the bottle up to my nipple, the scratchy white plastic against my skin. Milk began to dribble, then squirt. I filled half the bottle from one breast and the balance from the other. I put the milk in the fridge.

Carolina's squishy ghosts multiplied and took up residence in cupboards and frying pans and light bulbs. I worried that Carolina was stretching to some breaking point. I kept track as she developed what I called "personas." One was bouncy and energetic, an ordinary three-year-old. One was nervous and paranoid. Another resembled the ordinary child, but she walked starchily, talked hollowly and wore a determined plastic smile. Another was withdrawn into repetitive movements like rocking and dandling her blanket.

Searching for imagery to fit Carolina, I struck upon my clients, the strange, affectless men and women flapping their hands and spinning plates. While I knew three-year-old children did not simply "go autistic," autism found a sort of reflection in Carolina. Carolina was a lock. Autism was one of the keys I jiggled for fit.

Amy stopped smiling altogether. Her spells came frequently, two or three or five times a day and without warning. If I held her it was like holding cardboard; she was stiff. Sometimes she slapped and kicked and fought me off, entirely blind to the fact that I was her mother. About these spells I could do little. Gradually I learned my wisest response was just to stay near her, to avoid touching her, to whisper that things were fine. Amy, love, Mommy's here. Amy, sweetheart, Mommy's beside you. Eventually, after a half-hour or even an hour, her screams changed tenor and lost their nightmarish tone. Her eyes gradually cleared and focussed; then I could pick her up and bring her close. Amy, alert, was a monkey. She had a thorough way of cuddling in.

When Amy was three and a half months old, she cut two teeth within hours of each other. A day or two of drool and crankiness and out pushed two tiny pearls from her bumpy pink gums. I believed teething was an explanation for her problems. She was young for it, extremely young—though I'd heard that occasionally infants were born with teeth—and though she hadn't exhibited symptoms concurrently with her terrors, I felt she'd been in pain, unbeknownst to me, for months. I ran my idea by everyone I knew.

It was another key, like looking at autism. The fit in the lock wasn't awful. And I had little else. It was either teething or me, somehow me.

When Amy was four months old she began to fly off my breast by arching and propelling herself backwards, shrieking. Her cries raged over the dike of my love for her, capsizing me into a furious need for silence. It was her spells again, but worse. It would start either when she saw my nipple approach her mouth or later, partway through nursing, when she'd throw herself backwards so swiftly I was not always able, even anticipating it, to get my hand in place so she didn't crash into the arm of my chair. To assuage my guilt at leaving her to go to work, I expressed my breast milk, which meant that while I fed her from one breast, I held a bottle under the other and massaged myself. Juggling Amy and the bottle was like feeding twins. I had to fill at least four bottles a day. Worried my milk might begin to dry up, as it had with Carolina when I returned to work, I froze extras; in the kitchen freezer were row on row of what looked like foggy blue ice-water bottles.

One afternoon while I was expressing and Amy was sucking, she catapulted. I moved to catch her. The bottle fell. The milk I'd expressed dumped onto Amy's sleepers and my clean slacks and puddled on the carpet. Now I'd be late for work. Carolina was still napping. I was at my wits' end. I started to weep, mumbling to myself that I did everything I could think of but my kids only got worse. There was nothing normal in this. I tried to get Amy back on my breast. She flung off. Suddenly I knew what I wanted to do. I wanted—more than I could remember wanting anything—to hurl her across the room.

I rose sharply and walked her in circles, jiggling her. Amy, my wet, howling bundle, I thought, how have we come to this?

None too gently I spilled her into her crib and dragged myself outside. It was cold. The street was empty. I sat in a chair on the porch, pulled up my knees and rocked myself as Carolina sometimes rocked herself. I could still hear Amy's wails through the door.

I felt green and sick. I wasn't stupid—I understood that I wouldn't, couldn't have hurt Amy. But for a moment I'd seen her dashed brains dragging down our wall and loved it. Kids were parasites, I thought, who required the body of a mother to feed from, each pound stolen from hers, each skill wrenched from her storehouse of knowledge. I thought, It's not an umbilical cord that attaches us but a hose, a water main, with me at one end and the girls at the other. They're junkies. They have only to stir from sleep to mainline me like heroin.

I sat on a stool in front of Frank's chair and put a hand on his knee.

He stared at me. I saw his resentment: Ellen, Ellen, go away.

"I know you're beat. I know it's late. But there's something wrong with the kids."

Frank blinked.

"I think they need help," I continued. I hadn't formulated what the next step might be—therapy?—but I was saying it out loud, at least. "Frank, maybe I'll get a referral from the community centre, find someone who works with young children. Carolina's almost autistic, I swear. And Amy ... " I shook my head.

Frank stiffened and his expression chilled. I let my hand fall and sat up straighter.

He said, "You think *I* did it?"

"What?" I asked, puzzled. "Did what?"

He repeated himself. "Ellen, if you think *I* did it, you're crazy."

"Did *what*? What are you talking about?"

"I don't see what Carolina's got to complain about. She's got a great life. She's got it easy. You're not pinning this on me."

"Nothing's been *done* to Carolina. That's not what I'm talking about."

Frank searched the air to the side of my face. "Carolina has everything," he said atonally. "I've given both of them everything."

"I know you have," I said softly.

Frank bolted up and brushed past me. He paced, hands in pockets. "You think Carolina's got problems, Ellen? You think Amy does? Those kids don't have a worry in the world. Uh-uh." He stopped and turned to face me. "The nuns locked *me* in a cupboard when I was four."

I knew Frank had been affected by his early Catholicism. But I had not ... I had not what? What was he saying? What had happened to him? I imagined photographs of Frank small and vulnerable. Nuns? I thought. Nuns? Frank at four, in nursery school? Locked in a cupboard because he'd been bad? I unfolded from the stool.

Frank slammed out the door. He revved his truck, sending a plume of blue smoke under the streetlight.

I stood holding the door jamb, staring miserably after him.

6

I TIPTOED AROUND FRANK. I wanted badly to tell Brigit what he'd told me, but I was Frank's confidante and didn't want to violate his privacy. Clearly what I'd heard was all he was prepared to say. He wouldn't elaborate. But if nuns had locked Frank in a closet, what else? What else had happened to him?

And what did it mean when he said, "Ellen, if you think *I* did it, you're crazy"? What was the "it"?

I signed up for parenting classes. I went twice a week to those and once a week to a consciousness-raising group. I signed both Frank and me up for a couples' parenting class. Each week at seven on Thursdays, my day off, I dragged him to a Lutheran church basement where we could talk to other young parents and vent our frustrations. He was sullen during the sessions. He didn't speak on the way there or after we were home except once to say he thought the group a waste of time. After four weeks he called me to say he had to work late; we never returned.

But I was able, now, to be more patient with my kids. I began using effective communication skills; if these didn't help Carolina and Amy, they at least caused me to listen more carefully and that, in turn, soothed the girls.

I also called Frank's parents and my mother to see if I could discover something in our family histories, some rare disease that might account for Amy's symptoms. I'd had her back at the doctor to report that she now gagged and choked during her spells and to have the dark, baggy circles under her eyes examined. I'd taken her for anemia tests, holding her tight as a technician pierced her tiny foot to get a blood sample. Nothing in our family tree turned up obscurities; her anemia test was negative.

Even though our relationship was getting steadily worse, I still felt it was important to go through the motions of pleasing Frank. He only wanted sex once a week, on Sundays, and I went along. I counted the dots on the ceiling tile. Frank was so quick I never got past fifty. Week after week, that was my goal: to reach fifty-one. Not because I wanted him to last—by now the only good thing about having sex with Frank was how fast it was over—but because I wanted to see if he could.

Brigit had a new boyfriend. Just like Frank, he ejaculated prematurely.

I asked, "How's his ego? Frank's got an ego as thin as paper." The TV was tuned to "Mister Rogers." I looked at Carolina sitting cross-legged on the carpet. "He used to … uh … do foreplay, but Jesus, not once since Amy was born. Don't you hate it? I lie there hating it."

Brigit, who had Amy stretched along her legs, was making spider motions above her, then coming in for tickles. She looked up and said she and her boyfriend were in the honeymoon phase.

"Sex matters," I said. "Doesn't it matter?"

"Bruce does everything I want him to. The second time he's not so fast." Brigit smiled as Amy giggled.

"I hate sleeping with Frank," I said. "Sometimes I think it's my fault, like if I knew how to inspire him… " I felt tears welling. "It's just… I feel so desperate. Sex with Frank was never great, but I didn't used to mind so much. And I can't *tell* him, I can't say, 'Did I ever mention you're lousy in bed?'"

"That would go over big," Brigit said. She held Amy's feet and clapped them together, playing pattycake. "Have you ever considered saying no?"

I frowned. Refuse? I'd never, not once, considered refusing. I could refuse? "He'd think I don't love him."

Brigit looked up. "Do you?"

I couldn't decide on an answer.

"Well?"

I stared at Brigit hard. "Sometimes I'm *scared* of him," I said hesitantly. "Isn't that ridiculous?"

The thing was, there was a side of Frank his friends never glimpsed. He was sometimes sunk in depressions so deep he could send forth only grunts. Around me his voice was often laced with derision and contempt.

Frank was subterranean. No one saw below his surface. Even I only saw hints. He was lost inside himself. I sometimes worried that he was stoking some terrible fire, bottling up flammable gasses. But I didn't know how to say all this to Brigit.

Brigit spoke to Amy in baby talk. Finally she said, "If you're scared, you're scared."

After that, I had sex with Frank three more times. I was still ashamed of feeling repulsed when he touched me and of my secret but growing wish for a separation. I believed what most people had implied—that Frank was a saint to take me back after our split.

But I finally said no. No more sex.

I sat him down and told him plain out, rushing through my sentences, that I was not prepared to continue having sex with him. He didn't say anything. I waited. I waited some more. Finally he got up and walked away.

Frank asked just twice, a week and a half later and two days after that. No, I said, resolute.

I thought Carolina needed more stimulation. I was so often busy nursing, cleaning the house or working at the group home that I was slighting her. She was bored.

The place I found was in a cavernous hall near a hospital. Over two weeks, Carolina and I visited six times. There were sand trays, easels and paints, plastic blocks—these Carolina shyly played with. Gradually I backed farther and farther from her sphere of attention until, at last, she'd moved from discomfort to enthusiasm. She called the daycare "school"; she wanted to go.

Her first full day fell on a Thursday. I dropped her with her Sesame Street lunch pail and blanket at 9:00; I'd retrieve her at 3:30.

I took Amy to the country and carried her along the path of a dike. It was late autumn and chilly; in the pack on my back Amy was quiet. When water birds flushed from the marsh below us, screeching, Amy startled. I pulled her free and sat, holding her on my lap. Her hands clenched and unclenched; she wanted to move and touch.

I nursed her. I wrapped her in a thick blanket, covering her head. She suckled easily and wanted more; I switched breasts. I felt an aching loneliness while she drained my milk.

When Amy slipped off my nipple, asleep, I looked down on her tiny, upraised face. Her features were broad and sweet; a small dribble of milk sat at one corner of her lips. I tried to see into her. Her life had a grip on her and was pulling her up, lengthening her, strengthening her legs; soon she would sit in a puddle of buttery sun on our kitchen floor and try to grasp the dust floating in the air around her. Soon she would crawl and talk and walk. Then who knew? Anything could happen. I bent and kissed her forehead.

We went for Carolina just after 3:00. I had been at loose ends. The child I was used to tending, whose hair I braided, whose meals I cooked, whose skinned knees I bandaged: I wanted her back.

I tiptoed past the boots and coat racks to Carolina's classroom, stopped at the door. The kids were blasting into everything, a blizzard of legs and arms. I couldn't see Carolina. Then I noticed her in a corner with her blanket over her head.

A teacher saw me and told me Carolina had been upset since nap-time. She handed me a folded painting Carolina had done. I walked to Carolina's side and knelt down. "It's Mommy," I told her quietly. "Honey, Mommy's here."

Carolina slowly pulled the blanket from her head and stared at me with such a mixture of anguish and joy I caught my breath. Her eyes were red-rimmed; tears tracked down her flushed cheeks.

"Let's go, okay? Let's go home, sweetie pie." I helped her to her feet. "Do you want to tell me what happened?"

Carolina shook her head.

Later, at home, when I was starting dinner and Carolina was working with Play-Doh at the table, she said, "Mommy, how come you did that?"

I turned from the stove. Her tone was accusing. Her blue eyes were sharp as ice. "What?"

"Why did you leave me at school overnight? You said you'd come back to get me. You promised."

My mind did a flip. Overnight? "I didn't . . . " Then I understood. I pressed my fingertips to my forehead. I knelt beside her and took her hands. "Oh, Carolina, honey, I didn't leave you overnight. See the clock? It's five. It's the afternoon of the very same day I took you there. I dropped you in the morning. After lunch I came and picked you up."

"No, you didn't," she said. "We had to go to bed. It was night."

"Sweetheart, you just had a nap," I said. "It's because the nap room is downstairs and all the windows are covered up that you thought it was night. When you wake up from a nap here you can see it's still daylight, but at daycare I'll bet it's pretty dark. Was it dark when you went downstairs?"

"It was really, really dark," Carolina whimpered. "I didn't know why you wouldn't come to get me. Me and Blankie were scared. Me and Blankie thought you forgot us."

"C'mere," I said. Carolina climbed down off her chair and into my lap. She curled in tight. "It's a big promise, Carolina. I'll never leave you at school overnight. Cross my heart. I'll never forget you." I rocked her and kissed the top of her head until I felt her body loosen.

That night when I was getting Carolina ready for bed, I came across the painting from daycare. I thought we could put it up on the fridge, but when I unfolded it I gasped. The large page was covered with black paint, black angry slashes and swirls. Carolina asked if I liked it. I stumbled out, "Sure," but she knew I didn't.

She said, "I have witches inside me, you know. Just like Daddy."

≈

1965

I'm Mom's favourite. It's our secret. We don't tell Laurence and Margaret. But that's how come Mom says she'll take me to the divorce, so I can testify against Dad. Because she loves me best.

≈

I craved the consolation of a warm body. I knew Teresa's ex-husband Barry well, since their daughter, Samantha, and Carolina were best friends and Barry had a sort of loose, joint custody with Teresa; he and I liked each other. Barry had cashed in on the Vancouver real estate boom, buying houses low and selling high. He was also an artisan who designed and built furniture. Any time we spoke—as the girls played underfoot—Barry doodled, filling pages with strange, elaborate sketches.

In December, Barry kissed me. The girls were almost impossible to round up; Barry and I stood close and wordless. I said, "Barry, I—" but he covered my mouth with his lips.

When in another minute the girls appeared, like they had radar, we broke guiltily apart.

It was nearly Christmas. My brother Laurence called from the Sunshine Coast to say that he and his new girlfriend Marlise would join us. Frank's brother Dennis and Dennis's wife

Eleanor were already scheduled, so we would be eight; on the phone I laughed at something Laurence was saying. Carolina grabbed the phone cord. She pulled it farther into the room until I leaned forward. I spoke sharply to her but she knew she had the upper hand; I wasn't likely to get off. And I couldn't easily get up since I was nursing Amy.

I was asking Laurence about Marlise—was it serious?—when Frank appeared. I was half off my chair glaring at Carolina when Frank told her to stop.

Carolina ignored him.

"Never mind," I said to Frank and then to my brother, "What?"

Frank told Carolina to let the phone cord go.

Carolina gave no indication that she'd heard him. She'd wrapped the cord around herself and was giggling, pulling me closer.

Then Frank kicked her. He kicked her once in the leg, then, when she crumpled, in the side. Carolina wailed. Frank grabbed her, untangled her and carried her off.

I said, "Laurence, I'll call you back."

"No, wait," he said. "So Marlise wanted me to—"

I cut him off and slammed down the phone. I plunked Amy, who could now support herself, on the floor. I yanked a red musical apple between her legs.

"Frank?" I called. "Frank?"

I wanted to go to Carolina, but Frank stood outside her room barring the door.

"You kicked Carolina," I said, horrified.

"She wasn't listening."

I said, "You didn't need to interfere. It didn't involve you."

"She was rude."

"But you *kicked* her." She'd only fallen from surprise, though; his foot had hardly grazed her. "You can't kick Carolina. Adults can't kick children."

"I wanted to hit her, okay? But I didn't."

He stepped away from Carolina's door.

≈

1965

In divorce court I try to be invisible, sinking down on the hard bench beside Mom, but then one of the men up front calls my name. I have to go up into a box and remember which hand is my right hand and put it on a Bible and swear to tell the truth.

"Is it a fact that you sometimes don't have enough to eat?"

I look at the man but don't answer. I look past him and see another man. I frown and keep looking.

"Well, Ellen?"

The man who's talking sounds mad. The other man smiles.

"Is that my dad?" I ask, pointing to the smiling man. It's a year or so since I've seen him because I refuse to go on visiting weekends.

But it is. It is him. I wiggle in the box. He's staring at me. He won't stop staring at me.

≈

I was way too busy during the holidays. I worked a lot; we had a house full of company. Twice I napped in the early afternoon, and one day, when the girls were sleeping, Frank joined me. I was nervous he'd want sex, but he didn't; gradually I relaxed and slept. Carolina woke us by walking on her knees in the alley between our legs till we were forced apart. "Get apart," she sang. "Oh, Daddy and Mommy, get apart."

"Hi," I mumbled. "How was your nap?" I raised myself up and pulled her in for a hug.

Frank groaned and turned his back.

Carolina shimmied away, sitting cross-legged between us. She said, in a singsong voice, "Somebody's going to get hurt here."

"Huh?"

She said it forcefully. She was frightened. "Get up before somebody gets hurt, Mommy. C'mon, get up. Get up, Mommy."

"What do you mean, Carolina? Who's going to get hurt?"

"Somebody. Get up, get up." She pulled my arm.

"Nobody's going to get hurt, Carolina. Mommy and Daddy are just having a nap."

"No, no, no," she said. "Somebody's going to."

I gave in and pulled on my robe. Carolina followed me out. I asked her why she thought someone was going to be hurt, and who, but she couldn't or wouldn't explain. Maybe she'd seen Frank and me making love at some point? But that stretched belief. Our sex had been so quick and furtive it was unlikely Carolina had been even slightly aware of it.

Laurence and Marlise came in from the kitchen to say they'd made lunch—bagels with cream cheese and lox—so I dropped it. "Hungry, chum?" I asked Carolina.

She nodded.

I quit my job just after New Year's. One of my clients was becoming dangerous and it was no longer a relief to go to work; instead I was frightened. When my client blackened my eye and put his head through his bedroom wall, I gave my notice.

To celebrate the fifth anniversary of my move back to Canada and my reunion with Frank, he and I went to a restaurant in Stanley Park. It was not the kind of evening we were accustomed to. We sat under a skylight; outside the windows boats bobbed in the harbour. I wanted to leave Frank but had promised myself that if there was to be another split between us, he would have to initiate it. Then I'd be free. Then I could say to friends and family, shaking my bewildered head, "He left me. He just up and left me," and the onus would be on him.

I said, "Frank. Five years. It's astonishing."

He raised his wine glass as if to toast me. Since I didn't drink, I lifted my coffee cup and extended it. "To you," Frank said.

"To us," I corrected and smiled. "Who would have thought?"

Frank sat back.

"Frank," I said, leaning forward. I was nervous about what I wanted to say. "If we're going to do this, go on with this, I think we need to make a commitment to each other."

Frank stared at me through half-lidded eyes.

I faltered but continued because it was necessary. "This is important. I'm not talking marriage. I'm simply saying things aren't great between us. I'm recognizing that. We need to work on this." Or quit, I thought but didn't say.

Frank said, "Okay."

"Okay what?" Why did talking to Frank have to be so hard?

"Sure," he said, "okay."

"Like get couple counselling," I said. "Individual counselling. Things so we're communicating."

"I said all right."

"All right?"

Frank nodded.

It wasn't much, but maybe it was enough. Maybe we could learn how to be happy together? For the kids?

7

I HELD BRIGIT'S arm till she stopped walking. "I dunno," I said. I could see women clustered on the steps of the dance hall.

"C'mon," she said, laughing.

I let her haul me inside. There were dozens, maybe hundreds of women here. On the dance floor some were embracing. I pulled Brigit off to the side.

"We're not lesbians," I told her.

"Dance with me," Brigit said.

I shook my head. Some of the women around us were kissing.

"I won't bite," Brigit said, laughing and pulling me out onto the floor.

"Who leads?"

"I'll lead," Brigit said.

As we danced, I looked out over Brigit's shoulder.

"Relax," Brigit said in my ear.

But when I did, all I noticed was the feel of her breasts against me and how good she smelled. "I thought Frank was going to kill me when I said I was going to a women's dance."

Brigit held me closer.

"Doesn't Bruce mind?"

Brigit shrugged. Then she spun me out, surprising me.

≈

1966

What I know about lesbians is two of my girlfriends, Becky Harding and Sue Miller, who, during an all-girl spin-the-bottle session, practising for boys, kiss each other.

"Lezzies! Lezzies!" we shout.

≈

1968

I fall in love with boys all right. But the first time I have sex, in a shed with my boyfriend, Billy, I don't realize he's been inside me. I don't feel a thing.

I feel things with my best friend Elise, though. I kiss her and take nude photographs of her, leaving off her head so no one can identify her.

≈

1974

During university in New York, my best friend is a hilarious redhead named Madrigal. I meet her at the department store where we both work. She's in men's wear. She gets herself in the suit rack, hidden, her arm down a suit sleeve, and when a customer walks by she reaches out and grabs him, shouting, "Buy me!"

I'm wild by proxy. Madrigal and I choose men for her to seduce. We pick a guy, go on a leopard-skin-underwear buying spree, and Madrigal takes him to bed Saturday night. She sticks a tape recorder under her bed, and on Sundays, on her rooftop, we drink martinis and play the tape back, howling with laughter.

≈

Though Frank and I weren't having sex, I decided to have a tubal ligation. I was *not* going to have another child, period.

Not if Frank and I slept together again, not if we broke up and I was with Barry or someone else. I thought of kids in the dozens, as if they'd just happen no matter what I did.

Frank didn't seem to care. If he had feelings about it, he was keeping them to himself.

I booked an appointment.

In late January, on a Friday morning, I had Frank drop me at the hospital's surgical daycare unit. I wanted him to say something, anything, like, Ellen, please reconsider, but he did not. As I waited, I thought of the children I was forgoing, but how could I see them clearly? They were like spots across the sun, remote and nebulous. A tubal was ... protection. I was already stretched too thin, and still I sometimes wanted another. Have a baby, have a baby, have a baby, I thought with scary regularity.

By five, I was home. I was groggy, and the only evidence that I was sterile were two Band-Aids on my abdomen. Brigit, who was caring for the girls over the weekend, had fetched me, I knew, though I had no memory of her, no memory of the drive from the hospital or anything that had gone before.

I was still nauseous and headachy Sunday evening, but I was up looking after the girls. As I was preparing their supper, Frank, who'd been to a weekend men's group at my urging, told me he thought therapy was a waste of time.

"Did you meet anyone you liked?"

"Guy named Ted," he said.

I waited.

"We're going for beers Tuesday after work."

"Good," I said.

Frank said, "Ted beats his wife." He paused. "The counsellor said I don't have any problems, by the way."

I rolled my eyes so he couldn't see.

"When's dinner?"

I carried grilled cheese sandwiches to the table. "Dinner," I said, passing a plate to Carolina and another with a sandwich cut in tiny bits to Amy in her highchair, "is whenever you make it."

"You aren't cooking?"

"I didn't know what time you'd be home. There's cheese and bread on the counter."

I coaxed Amy to try her sandwich. I was more and more concerned about her diet; she never let me feed her. My attempts to put food close to her mouth sometimes sent her into a spell. She hardly ate. Not fruit or any vegetable. No meat. Not yogurt or cheese. She liked cereal with milk, buttered toast and crackers, apple juice. After I stopped nursing her, I'd put her on formula so she'd get some nutrition.

"Yum," I said to Amy, gobbling one of her bits.

Amy slammed her hand down on her plate and sent the sandwich bits flying to the floor.

"Damn it, Amy." I got up shakily. To Frank I said, "I have to go back to bed. I'm dizzy."

"God knows I'm used to that," he said.

A few days later I was feeling fine. I said to Barry, "I'm changing my name. I'm tired of having my father's name. Billings. What kind of name is Billings? Every time I hear it I wince."

Barry smiled.

"I'm taking my mother's birth name, Prescott. Frank thinks I'm crazy. Maybe he's right, but I don't care."

"Ms. Prescott, if you were crazy, I wouldn't be sitting here thinking how pretty your lips look," said Barry.

Which effectively sidetracked me.

In early March Frank came home and told me he'd rented an A-frame cabin at Whistler, a small community just over a hundred kilometres north of Vancouver.

I was mending seams in a stack of clothing. "What?"

"For April first."

I bit through a piece of knotted thread. "Frank, could you please repeat yourself?"

"I rented a cabin at Whistler."

I had the picture of our anniversary dinner, a short month

and a half earlier, firm in my mind. Maybe he meant he'd rented a studio. "For April first," I said, "and?"

"I'm moving up there."

"You're moving to Whistler," I said dangerously. I picked up a pair of his jeans with a missing button. "You're leaving me?"

"You don't want to move up there, Ellen. You'd hate it up there. I got a job on a dude ranch. I already gave notice in Abbotsford."

I folded a shirt of Carolina's. "Frank, wait a minute. You're leaving us?" My voice was shrill.

"The job came available and a guy there knew about this cabin."

He was moving out? I had two little kids and three weeks—three *weeks*—to find a place to live? "But isn't this the sort of thing we should discuss? I mean, you can't just walk in here and say, Ellen, the jig's up. You can't do that, Frank. What about the girls?" I threw his pants down.

"Well, I mean," he said, "you can come if you want."

"To *Whistler*?"

"I knew you wouldn't."

It was simple to get involved with Barry. After Frank's announcement, I slipped over the edge and into Barry's bed. I had one absolute rule: if there were kids with us, no sex, not even if they were asleep. Otherwise, what did I care? The sex was great. I'd been a long time wanting sex to be good.

I found a reasonably priced basement suite in East Vancouver. It had only one bedroom, but I could sleep in the living room on a pull-out sofa. I reapplied for welfare, but they wouldn't give me benefits. I qualified for unemployment insurance. I was looking for a job, right? Right? I nodded, too ashamed to admit I wasn't.

I found it harder and harder to get Carolina to daycare by the nine o'clock deadline. On Thursday, a week before we were to move out (on April first—April Fools' Day, I thought), I slept in. Frank shook my shoulder.

"Why didn't you wake me?"

It was nearly 8:30. I had twenty minutes. The daycare was already threatening suspension for prior lateness; it interfered with their program to have a child come late. Frank was dressed. I groaned. "Can't *you* take her?"

His eyes narrowed.

"Just this once?" I said. "Please?"

Frank walked out of the room. I took it as a no and yanked on jeans and a sweatshirt. I stumbled to the kitchen and stood to run water for coffee. I held the edge of the sink. Frank was across the kitchen making his lunch. I could hear Carolina in her bedroom; I hoped he'd fed her and gotten her dressed, at least.

"I—"

When I turned, Frank's face was contorted and red. There was anger in it, hatred and rage. His eyes were slits. He clutched a butcher knife. His body vibrated. I noticed that; his body and his black hair looked electrical.

"Want—" he slurred.

I couldn't move. I was rooted to the spot. The water ran.

"To—kill—you." He spat the words.

I swallowed. He raised the knife. Sun glinted on the blade. The knife cut the air and skittered into the sink in front of my fingers, clattering. Frank gave a sort of parched scream, then bolted. I looked at the water splashing over the knife. I clung to the sink, my knees shaking.

As my senses returned, I noticed Frank hauling Carolina away. Wobbily, I followed. I pulled open the front door. From the cab of the truck, Carolina smiled and waved. I moved my lips, my hand—smile, wave.

I called Carolina's daycare. I said I had the flu and that Frank was bringing Carolina but the truck had faulty brakes and I was worried. "Isn't she there?" I repeated. "Isn't she there yet?" The alternative—that Frank might finish with Carolina what he'd started with me—turned my sweat cold.

On my fifth call, she was there.

I fed Amy as if I were a ghost mother, put her down in toys and packing boxes. I made coffee. I scrubbed the toilet, the sink, the tub. On my hands and knees, I washed the bathroom floor. I washed the breakfast dishes, drying the butcher knife and dropping it into its slot in our knife rack. I made the beds and tidied the living room.

I watched Amy, but it was as if I had no connection with her; she banged and rolled and bit her toys and I was only conscious of noticing, of seeing.

I called Brigit and Teresa and Jean, but no one was home. I called my mother. I began to cry when she answered. "Mom, a knife," I blubbered. "A butcher knife. It missed me by just inches." I couldn't explain Frank's face, how it had been a mask of evil. "He said he wanted to kill me."

"I'm sure Frank didn't mean it, dear," Mom said. To someone else she whispered, "My daughter." Then, to me, "Frank's got a lot on his mind. Frank has a lot to worry about, supporting you and two kids."

"Mom," I said, groping for a response.

"I have to go, Ellen. I have company."

I gave in. "Right. Okay. Right, bye."

"How are the girls?"

"The girls are fine, Mom."

"I'll talk to you soon, then."

"Right," I said.

When my mother was bad, she was horrid.

For the next week, I tiptoed around Frank, trying to do everything right, grateful for the upcoming move which meant I did not have to question or confront what he'd done. Still, I reacted to it again and again. It replayed itself in my brain, etching there as if onto stone. I'd find myself stalled, lost in terrified thought, and only shaken back out when one of the girls screamed.

After the move, I was deeply relieved not to have to watch Frank warily, wondering when his murderous rage might erupt again, but I also felt that the kids and I were broken bits, shards carved off a flank. This was the hard part of losing Frank. Frank was our authenticity. I could not see the three of us as a whole, as a "family."

I was also terrified. I was living on my own in a damp basement apartment, with scarcely any money and two quite troubled children. I felt overwhelmed and lonely.

When Frank made overtures a few weeks later, I was ready to put aside my fear and befriend him. He started to come around a lot. Besides taking the girls weekends and sometimes Carolina on a Wednesday night, he dropped in for frequent visits. He talked to me a little, opened up. Soon he had a girlfriend. I supported him, ignoring tinges of what I considered irrational jealousy.

One afternoon, conversationally, he told me he'd wanted to kill me the first time we broke up.

I really didn't believe Frank was violent. Despite the knife incident, about which he had never commented beyond a grunted apology, I was convinced that he couldn't hurt a fly. Or so I repeated to myself again and again. When I worried about the girls being with him at the mountain, I told myself it was because of his girlfriend. I told myself Frank was a sweetheart. Everybody thought so.

He gave me a small bit of child support money and sometimes brought groceries. I had breaks from parenting. What more could I ask for?

I held my head barely above water.

I carried Amy to the girls' bedroom. Carolina, who was supposed to be dressing for her fourth birthday party, was lying naked on her bed with her legs in the air, fingering and pulling at herself.

"Come and play, Mommy," she warbled.

"Carolina," I said, "get dressed."

"I'm having a game."

"Carolina," I repeated, "get dressed. It's party day."

"Are you bad, Mommy?"

I was distracted. I kept trying to curtail Amy long enough to get her into a diaper and tights. "What?"

"'Cause you won't play with me?"

I said, "Honey, you have *friends* coming." I let Amy go with just her dress and diaper on.

"Is my dad coming?"

"He'll be here soon."

Carolina chanted, "The mommy mouse and the baby mouse are okay, but the daddy mouse is going to come and get me out of my bed and take me into the walls where there are no windows and no one will ever be able to get me out again."

"Carolina," I said sternly. "If you're not in that dress in two minutes ..."

"Black stain one. Black stain two. Black stain in a pot with you."

I rose and frowned. She was bouncing on the side of her bed. "Don't you want to have a party, honey?"

"Big girl birthday," she sang. "Birthday in a pot with you!"

"Do you want to wear your blue dress, instead?"

Carolina grabbed her red and white dress and pulled it over her head.

Later, when the kids were eating cake out in the backyard, I drew Teresa aside and told her what Carolina had been chanting about mice. "We've *got* mice," I considered. "Carolina sees mice here all the time."

"It's the breakup," Teresa said firmly, squeezing my shoulder. "She's scared about mice and about her daddy leaving."

"I know. I thought of that. But Teresa, I can't help thinking there's something I'm missing, something that's obvious."

"Carolina seems fine to me," Teresa said. Her little son Daniel was pulling himself up on a stone ledge and doing something close to knee bends.

"Yeah," I said, "she's fine." I watched Carolina. "She's fine, I'm sure."

≈

1961

Daddy takes me to the Hunt Club for riding lessons. Sometimes there are new puppies in the kennel, but one time he takes me into the barn and lifts me high up to see inside a vat. I see hot bubbles of pink foam and then horses. Horses' hoofs and horses' knees and a horse's head with an empty eye socket. Parts bob up and sink back down. Daddy's holding me up by the crotch.

Daddy says, "That's how they make dog food, Ellen."

"Put me down! I want down!"

Daddy says, "That's also where bad little girls who talk too much go. You're not a bad little girl, are you, Ellen?"

≈

Oh, Amy, I thought, oh, Amy, munchkin. I pulled myself from bed at the sound of her shrieks and gags. I hung over her crib, found her soother, in the blankets, helped her hand close around it and directed it gently towards her mouth. If I was very slow and lucky, she'd take it, suck, and the spell would end—she'd fall asleep. More and more often, though, she'd thrash around to avoid the soother, continually spitting it out.

Her terrors never bothered Carolina. Carolina went about business as usual while Amy screamed and choked. If she was watching "Sesame Street," she'd just turn up the volume. My voice, trying to reach Amy, could hardly be heard over the din.

"Amy, sweetheart, Amy, honey, it's okay, it's okay. Mommy's here, sweetie. Mommy will keep you safe. Everything's fine, sugar. Wake up now, honey. C'mon, pumpkin, wake up." I always wondered, in the hours I sat beside her crib or lay beside her on the floor, if Amy in a spell saw images or heard sounds. She was in a world of her own—she didn't hear "Sesame Street" or me—but did she hear something else? See something else?

As for Carolina, she drove me batty. On the hour she had some new, creative complaint. "My finger's broken," she'd say sadly, or "My toe needs to go to the hospital." "I can't walk, Mommy. My knee, my knee!" Each time she heard a new word for breakage—"detonate," say—she'd incorporate it. "My elbow feels like it's going to detonate." I spent a ridiculous amount of time kissing things better.

Carolina still feared mice, and she'd developed a morbid anxiety about fire. My insistence that we were safe didn't help. "Mice can start fires," she told me. I said they could not. "The daddy mouse can so," she said. I thought of mice gnawing on electrical wiring. "No," I said, "it's impossible."

As the weeks passed, April then May, Carolina didn't want to leave me to go to her father's. All I could do was listen and sympathize as she tried to talk me out of sending her, as she built up to begging or gave up and exhibited her acquiescent, plastic façade. When Frank arrived, Amy caterwauled and Carolina yanked me aside for one last try. "Don't make me go, Mommy. Mommy, I beg you. I'll be good. I won't bother you. I'll stay in my room all weekend. I won't eat, even, please, just don't make me go."

Carolina had colours for the days of the week. Friday and Saturday were brown. Sunday was grey. Monday was yellow.

One Monday morning Carolina climbed into bed with me. She sat on my stomach, bouncing, and I groaned and turned away, dumping her. She jumped on my side. I noticed bruises on her upper inner thigh. I held her leg. "What are these?" I asked, pointing. There were four round bruises in a half circle, each as big as a dime. I pushed Carolina off and sat up.

Carolina shrugged. "Bruises."

"I see they're bruises. What I'm asking is where they're from."

"I dunno."

"They weren't here on Friday," I said. They were fresh, purply.

"Probably I fell," Carolina said.

"Well, they're very odd, Carolina. I can't imagine what you could fall on to give you bruises that look like this. They're circles, honey. Circles in a half arc."

"Are you mad, Mommy?"

"Why would I be mad?"

" 'Cause I got bruises."

I sighed. "No, I'm not mad. Everybody gets bruises." I pulled her in for a cuddle. I stroked her temples. "Everything go okay at Daddy's?"

She nodded.

"You're sure, Carolina?"

"I'm happy it's yellow day," she said, snuggling in.

"Oh yeah, sugar. Me too."

Later that day, Carolina tore shrieking from the bathroom. "Mommy! Mommy! A bloodache!"

She led me to the toilet. Because of ghosts, Carolina never flushed. Flushing, she said, made ghosts come out. There was blood caught in nets of something slimy and white around her stool.

I phoned the doctor, who told me to watch very carefully and bring Carolina in if I saw blood again.

"Carolina, I need you to tell me if it happens again. Do you promise?" I said.

Gravely, Carolina promised.

≈

1963

"Mom can't really make us," Laurence says.

"Can too," I say, picking a scab.

"Uh-uh. Not if we ride off before he comes."

"He'll be mad. Laurence, we'll get spankings."

"Mom doesn't spank us."

"Dad does."

"We'll be gone. We'll ride to the Little League field. He won't look there. He can't drive on the grass."

Laurence is eleven. I am nine. Our little sister is only six. We take off; Margaret goes to Dad's alone and comes back hysterical and shaking so hard that Mom keeps her out of school for a week.

"Big baby," I tell her as she huddles in bed. She's been alternately staring out at nothing and shaking, for days. "You're a stupid baby."

But inside I am scared.

≈

I was out to dinner with the girls at a friend's house. I didn't know Simone well; she'd met me recently at a women's coffee-house and tucked me under her wing. Frank was due to pick up Carolina to take her to a baseball game at 7:00; at 6:30 I was called to the phone.

"Where are you?" Frank demanded.

"Frank," I said, "where are *you*? Where did you get this number?"

"I'm at your place. You're late. We said 6:30."

"How did you get *in*?"

"Your landlord let me in."

"My landlord did what?"

"Look, Ellen, we said 6:30. It's 6:30. When are you coming home?"

I took a deep breath. "I'll be there soon."

Though I told myself having Frank in my house was no big deal, all the way home I stewed. I felt violated, angry at Frank and angrier still at my landlord.

When I drove up, Frank was outside. As I got out of the car he passed me a folded piece of paper. I looked a question at him, then opened it slowly. It was from my landlord, evicting me. I sagged back against the car. "I'm evicted? He evicted a single mother and two little kids? After I've been here just two months?"

"He says his wife's parents are coming to Canada."

"July first?"

Frank unbuckled Carolina. Amy was sound asleep in her car seat. Frank passed me her wicker diaper bag.

Amy turned one the first week of June. She was making earnest, toddly efforts to walk now; she was adorable. Her hair, so long at birth, fell to her waist in curls. Her face was round, her eyes blue.

She didn't talk, though, except for the word "Mama." She didn't understand how to unwrap gifts. Carolina and her friend Samantha helped. Carolina also helped Amy blow out her candles. "See? See, Amy? You swallow air, then …"

We let Amy have a go. She didn't lean forward. She sat in her highchair and puffed ineffectually. We laughed. Amy looked insulted. She grabbed her soother and stuffed it in her mouth.

It seemed like such an ordinary day. I stood back watching my kids, watching Frank, and I made the birthday wish Amy could not: that things would stay exactly as they were forever.

8

THIS THAT WAS a hot spot inside me, this that sent up orange flares, this, this word, this well of a word, this one word. Brigit said it in her VW van as we drove home from the university after a lecture. Discussing her friend Susan, she said it: "Incest." How far could a coin drop? I waited. The word was glaringly bright, falling through the bottom of my body.

Brigit didn't notice. She went blithely on, telling me, telling me, while my palms soaked with perspiration and my knees trembled. I wanted her both to stop—it was urgent she stop, stop immediately, stop posthaste—and to go on, explicating my dread.

I didn't say, Brigit, stop the car. I only said, finally, quietly, as if it were the most natural request in the world, "Brigit, could I meet her? Susan? Could I meet Susan? Would she mind?"

After that I came unglued. I did the ordinary things on automatic pilot—cared for the girls, looked for an apartment—but even when I signed a lease for a one-bedroom east-end suite I hardly noticed. I didn't pack. My concentration was shot. I'd cook the girls the most instant meals I could imagine, like Kraft Dinner, then stare off into space until the noodles burned in the pot or cooled and congealed. Whatever had been unnerving me all these years was expanding inside me like a sponge dipped in water.

When Friday came, Carolina had a mild fever; only Amy went to the mountain with Frank. I spent the weekend in bed.

Carolina and I played Snakes and Ladders and Go Fish in the covers. We ordered pizza. I was happy enough to spend time with Carolina solo, but I was sick. In the mirror my eyes reflected back dully.

I set up an appointment with Brigit's friend Susan; she'd visit Saturday evening while Carolina was at the mountain. If she thought it was strange I wanted to meet her, to hear her tell her story, she didn't say so.

I couldn't get anything done. It was as if all my nerve endings were outside my skin, jangling. I was waiting. My father, dead now ten years, waited with me. Things between us—like games of gin rummy—rose before my eyes. I saw my father superimposed over images of myself like a blanket.

Was I insane?

I dragged myself like someone haunted through the next few days. Even the rudiments of social conversation were beyond me. I told Barry I couldn't see him. When Frank returned with Amy, I rushed him away.

Incest?

≈

1967

I sit in a side room reserved for immediate family at my father's funeral—he's killed himself at age forty-six—and observe the mourning crowd. I listen to the minister drone on. Why do people love my father so much?

I, for one, am almost glad he's dead. I know I should try to work up some tears—I'm his daughter, for God's sake, and people are watching me—but my eyes stay dry.

≈

I'd come completely unglued. I'd fallen asleep. Now I woke to the noise of Amy in the grip of a spell. I lurched to the bedroom. Amy's tiny head was pushed back; the small, wiry tendons on her neck bulged and strained. The rest of her body was flaccid, as if paralyzed and beyond her control. All the air in the world was available to her and her mouth was empty, but still she gagged and choked. She'd been like this since Monday when Frank returned her from the mountain. My hands clenched against the crib bars. For a split second as I stared at my convulsing daughter, not knowing why, I hated Frank. I turned and looked at Carolina, slumbering Carolina with her blistered crotch. I shook my head to clear it. I sagged and fell on my knees. *Should* I kill them? That's what I'd been thinking earlier. Should I string ropes from the ceiling and tie them around the girls' necks? I wanted to. All day I'd wanted to. Amy was crying loud as jackhammers. I could help her, though, couldn't I? I could put my hands on her throat and squeeze. I slammed my hands over my ears.

"Stop it," I whispered.

Finally, trembling, I managed to pull myself to the phone to call for help. Simone, my new friend, came over and sat with me until Carolina got up and Amy stopped howling.

To think of myself as homicidal then, propped up in my bed while Simone made sandwiches, seemed unreal and absurd. It was a normal, late June day. It was hot. I had practical problems, of course—the move a week away predominant among them—but otherwise things were calm and fine. Weren't they?

Weren't they? Thursday and Friday were nondescript. I was nervous, but nervousness and a kind of wariness were by now second nature. The kids were a distraction. I took them to the beach; I took them to a place called Scoopers for ice cream. They were so wild and hilarious and curious, their pale skin so translucent, their hair so shaggy, their eyes so blue that my breath caught in my throat, over and over. They charmed me. I felt very lucky, and if I was aimed like a bullet towards Saturday night when I would see—and interrogate—Brigit's friend Susan, I was also counting my two lucky stars, Carolina and Amy.

It was Carolina's weekend to go up to the mountain. Because Frank was planning to take her to see *Sesame Street*, the play, on Saturday afternoon, Carolina would only spend one night with him, not the usual two or three. We spent Saturday morning together weeding the landlord's garden while Amy toddled the yard; I knew I should be packing, but I was too distracted. Amy ate dirt. This child who would eat only cereal, crackers and toast put dirt and stones in her mouth. Carolina and I laughed as she spat out brown streaks of drool and small pebbles. "Poor sweetie," I said and pulled her onto my lap, wiping her chin with the corner of my T-shirt.

After lunch I reminded Carolina she needed to get ready for *Sesame Street*.

"No," she said.

"Honey, yes. Daddy will be here in an hour."

"I won't go, Mommy," she said.

"Don't be silly, Carolina." I put dishes in the sink. "You've been looking forward to this. You'll get to see Oscar and Big Bird. Don't you want to see Big Bird?"

"But Amy has to come," Carolina insisted.

"Daddy only has two tickets."

"You come, Mommy. I'll sit on your lap and Amy can sit on Daddy's and we'll only use up two seats."

"Carolina, they won't allow it. If there are two tickets that means two people. C'mon, into the shower." I guided her to the bathroom and turned on the water. I had her check the temperature. "This is your weekend alone with your daddy, Carolina. I thought you'd be happy."

"Samantha can come," Carolina said. "Okay? Sammy can come with me."

"No, hon, just you. Today's special just for you."

Carolina bolted from the bathroom, fell on her stomach, kicked her legs and pounded the floor with her fists. "I won't go!" she yelled. "You can't make me!"

I sat beside her. Carolina rarely had temper tantrums. She'd rarely had them when she was two.

"I won't go to Daddy's without Amy! There's snow!"

"Look," I said. "We're running out of time, Carolina. I'll tell you what. You go to *Sesame Street*, and afterwards I'll get Dad to bring you back here. How's that? If you still don't want to go to the mountain then, you can stay home. All right? Does that sound fair?"

Carolina sat up looking sheepish. Her cheeks were tear-stained. She nodded assent.

"Well, hurry," I said, growling and getting up on my hands and knees, "before the water turns cold." I chased her, giggling, into the bathroom.

When Frank arrived, Carolina clung to me. "Don't make me go," she whispered.

"She's been a little cranky," I told Frank. "She's not sure she wants to go up to the mountain. I told her you'd bring her home after the show so she can decide."

"Come on, Carolina," Frank said.

"Can you bring her back here?" Carolina was hiding her head.

Frank agreed he would.

"Daddy's bringing you home again. C'mon. Everything will be okay, you'll see. Maybe one of Big Bird's feathers will float off into the audience and you can bring it home to show me."

Finally Carolina filled her lungs with air, squared her shoulders and slipped off my lap. I picked up Amy. "Wave," I told the baby. "Wave bye-bye."

I started mechanically filling boxes. I resented the move. I felt vulnerable and resentful, resentful even of Frank's ability to take Carolina to a show. He had come to me, who could barely afford to feed the girls, who lived on a financial tightrope, enthusing that he'd saved $3000 in our nearly three months of separation. But *I* knew, if he didn't, that he'd saved it at his children's expense. Frank was oblivious, proud of his frugality. The only way I could counteract the kids' deprivation was to insist that he take them to the events I couldn't afford. He was talking about taking Carolina to Disneyland in October.

Amy was still napping when Frank and Carolina returned.

Carolina shoved paraphernalia into my arms. "I don't have to go to the mountain, right?" she said. "You said I don't have to go, Mommy."

"That's right, Carolina. Don't you want to?"

Frank said, "I'll think you don't love me."

I looked up at him, frowning. I didn't like blackmail. "No," I told Carolina firmly, "you can stay home."

"My feelings will be hurt," Frank said.

"Daddy will have hurt feelings," Carolina parroted.

"Daddy's a grownup," I said. "Frank, stop it. Will you just stop it?"

"Ellen," he said, "you always do this."

"Do what? This is Carolina's choice. I think she should stay home."

"You and your feminists," he said thickly.

"What on earth are you talking about?"

"Get your stuff," Frank said curtly to Carolina.

To Carolina I said, "What about it, pumpkin? You're welcome to stay home."

"No," she said. "I'll go. I guess I'll go."

"Honey?" I said, holding her chin and looking into her frightened eyes. "Are you sure?"

"Daddy needs me to," she said.

"That's no reason," I said. "You only go if you want to."

"I want to," she assured me.

"Just till tomorrow. Just one overnight."

Frank snatched up Carolina's bag and glared at me triumphantly.

Carolina threw her arms around my neck and held on tight. I gently extricated her. I said, falsely cheerful, "I'll see *you* tomorrow. Uncle Laurence is coming to visit. Maybe we'll make hamburgers on the barbecue. Give me a kiss." Carolina kissed me. "I'll miss you."

Carolina took her father's hand and walked out. She kept looking back over her shoulder to see me.

"I feel shy," I told Susan later that night. "I'm sorry. Because what I—because I want to pick your brain. The thing is, ever since Brigit told me she had a friend who—" I threw up my arms. "I've had this sinking sensation. I keep telling myself I must be crazy. I mean it's crazy, right? But it's like a sense of doom." I grinned, embarrassed. "It's as if I've been waiting for you. I know that sounds stupid. I'm supposed to move next week. But all I could think about is you and now you're here and I just feel silly."

Susan was a tall and wiry redhead, a student at a local community college. She had the angular grace of a dancer. She seemed to take up more room than just the chair she sat in across from me; she seemed to extend. "If I can help," she said, "I'm glad to."

"I'm sorry," I repeated. "I know this is really ridiculous. I didn't know who else to turn to."

"What do you want to know?"

"Well, what happened. And how you remembered. Brigit said you didn't remember? This sounds nosy. I mean, I haven't had a memory or anything. So how am I supposed to know if—?"

Susan sighed. I could see her steeling herself. She ran through things like a litany: "I felt like I was drowning. I had fears. Inexplicable fears. I hated to leave my apartment. I thought something was going to get me."

"Paranoia," I said, nodding. "I'm paranoid." I thought of earlier in the week, my conviction that I should kill my children.

"You know what one of my friends said? She said sometimes when we're paranoid we're not paranoid enough." Susan laughed. "Nobody else is going to be able to tell you if you've been sexually abused, Ellen. Nobody has that information except you."

"I already know I was," I heard myself saying.

Susan lifted her eyebrows.

I turned my hands over and over. "I've known since Brigit told me about you, Susan. I knew while she was talking. I just put it on hold. I didn't put words to it. But I can feel it. I don't know how to explain it. I haven't caught up, but my body knows. Does that sound stupid?"

Susan shook her head.

"I keep having this image of my dad's belly. And then I think of bologna. Like my dad's skin reminds me of bologna."

Susan looked at me tightly. "I always said my brother's skin reminded me of rubber."

"Oh God, Susan." I slumped in my chair. "The thing is, my dad's dead. He's been dead ten years."

Susan shrugged.

"I don't remember feeling anything for him but fear, you know, a sort of repulsion. Or nothing. I never think: Dad, good feeling. Dad and good feelings don't go together." I looked up, tentative.

"If he hurt you, Ellen, you don't need to feel guilty."

"I must have been pretty little. I never saw him after I was ten."

"Mine started when I was six. Then my father invited my brother to join."

"Six," I repeated, staring at her aghast. And then I heard, "No, I was younger."

"Younger?"

"Two," I said firmly.

"How do you know?" Susan asked.

"I peed my bed," I said, then I pushed up from the table and walked into the unrenovated part of the basement. I wasn't wearing shoes. The cement was cold. I walked in circles, holding my head. Susan touched my shoulder. I knew it was Susan. On some level I knew it was Susan, but her touch repelled me. I yanked away, looked at her and saw a faceless, plastic doll. I saw my father as if he were in the room with me, in my childhood bedroom. Talking. Touching me. Stroking my stomach. I saw my little sister's crib beside us. How old was I? Three? Four? It was dark, very dark. Then, very clearly, I saw Frank. The sight of him startled me back.

"I'm so scared," I told Susan. My teeth were chattering. "Please, will you stay with me? Please don't go."

"I'm not going anywhere," Susan reassured me. "I'll spend the night with you."

≈

1960

Dad buys each of us kids a calf. It's to teach us about business. Buy low, sell high. Mine, Brownie, is a day old, and I sit in his stall feeding him out of large glass baby bottles.

Later, a year before it's time, I come home from school for lunch and Brownie and the other calves are being loaded for slaughter. I run to Mom, but Dad is there. She waves me away. I pull on Dad, but he laughs.

≈

1961

I like my filly Louise. She's not really my filly, but I pretend she is. One day Daddy goes to get King, one of the stallions. I pull on my dad's pant leg, but he drags me, then kicks me off in the dirt. The stallion is big and mad. He snorts. Mommy runs out and yells, "That filly is too young! Too young!" and cries, but Daddy won't stop. The stallion high-steps, his ears pricked up. Daddy leads him by his bridle, opens the paddock gate, unsnaps his lead and slaps his haunch. The stallion prances in. His thing comes out big as Daddy's arm.

Mommy scoops me up.

Daddy's laughing.

Mommy runs me away. Her tears flick onto my face. "Cover your ears, Ellen."

But I still hear Louise screaming.

≈

1956

Skinned rabbits up high.

My father's big hand. "See these rabbits, Ellen?"

The rabbits have no skin.

"I killed them because they were getting into your mother's lettuce patch."

Red rabbits, up high, hanging.

Laurence has a good-luck white rabbit's foot.

"They were bad, Ellen." My father kneels down. "When little girls are bad, what happens?"

"Trouble," I mumble.

"That's right, that's why you're going to be good." My father looks up at the rabbits.

I do too. I look up. The rabbits have no skin.

"No more telling Mommy, right? No more. Do you understand?"

"No more," I say.

"I'll skin you alive, Ellen, if you tell. Do you understand?"

≈

The memories came hard and furious, in kaleidoscopic bursts. The hayloft, the attic, my bedroom. Everywhere my father, his redhead's skin, my face, his ropy big hand, my thighs, his oily forehead, my hand touching the mushroom-soft cap of his penis, which he exposed by pulling back his foreskin. Me peeing on his hand. Me sticky. The sight of his freckles. His smell like old cigars and hunger.

My father was the vice-president of a family construction firm. My father was well-respected. My father was admired. *One, two, unbuckle Daddy's ... Three, four, he shut the door.* Always a door, closing, no Mommy anywhere, just Daddy, Daddy, Daddy and Ellen, big as a popsicle, big as a doll, *Ellen, you're my special doll, aren't you, Daddy's doll, you understand me, don't you, Ellen, I can count on you, Ellen, that's it, baby.* Holding my head down, I can't breathe, can't can't can't—

Susan was curled up beside me on the bed, asleep. I peered around my night-dark apartment, checking the table, the fridge, the highchair.

Hate you, hate you, hate you, I heard, and my shoulders rounded. I felt itchy crinolines on my legs and had to scratch. Bobby socks. Patent leather shoes. My hair pulled into pigtails, tight. Cornflakes at the breakfast table. My father's chair, my father. I hyperventilated.

The phone rang. I bolted from bed and grabbed it up. "What? What?"

In bed, Susan stirred.

It was Brigit, Brigit crying. I tried hard to understand what she was saying, but I couldn't concentrate.

I gave Susan the phone. When she hung up she said, enunciating very clearly, "Brigit has had a fire in her bedroom. It's been put out but she'd like us to come over."

Brigit has had a fire, I repeated to myself. Struggling, I said, "A fire."

"I have to go over there. Are you coming?"

I found my clothes and pulled them on. Then I woke Amy. As we walked to the car I felt her grey elephant bang against my back.

Brigit lived near the hospital in a house with seven other students. Her bedroom, where the fire had started and luckily been contained, was on the attic floor. Called down to a late dinner, Brigit had left a candle burning. People clustered in the kitchen. No one knew what to do or say. The house smelled bitter. The doors were open, and fans pushed air around. Brigit led us upstairs. The landing walls were black. The third floor was wet from firefighters' hoses. In her room, Brigit bent to stacks of books and journals. Her clothes hung in scraps from a pole in one corner. She gathered charred armfuls up and carried them downstairs.

"Leave her," one woman advised.

Someone mentioned insurance adjusters. Someone else talked about water damage on the second floor. They asked how old Amy was. I wandered onto the porch. Brigit was down in the yard moving through the darkness, hanging her dresses on the clothesline. I sat on the steps. Amy toddled behind me.

A patch of light from a street lamp rounded the garage and formed a triangle on the yard. Sometimes Brigit stepped into it, illuminating her bare legs and a corner of her cotton gauze skirt.

I watched Brigit's arms like shadows as she pegged. I heard crickets. The night was warm. It seemed normal, except for this obviously wrong midnight activity. I thought of my father. I thought of my memory of urinating on my father's hand. I thought of Frank. I remembered the time early in our relationship when I'd wet his bed.

My father, Frank. Frank, Dad. Why couldn't I separate the two?

It was like submerging in a well, going down. The light dimmed.

Then I understood. The knowledge that I had been groping towards, what I'd rather have died than know, what killing my children would have prevented me from discovering, vibrated through me.

I sent it rattling towards my vocal cords. It hit the base of my skull.

Frank, I thought.

Frank is sexually abusing my daughter.

Carolina.

PART TWO

9

I PICTURED FRANK'S HOUSE, Frank's bedroom, how Carolina had said Frank sometimes had her sleep with him. I pictured Carolina in Frank's bed. A good image, Carolina in her nightie curled up beside a sleeping Frank. A bad image, Frank bending— I tried to cut it off. But it sizzled in my arms and fingers, my calves and toes, electric. White-knuckled, I clenched the stair. Frank? I thought. Blue flames; waves of nausea rolling like lava.

The landscape of my mind exploded; detritus fell everywhere. Carolina fell, tumbling and burning and breaking.

My Carolina.

I mumbled something.

In the yard, Brigit was hugging herself, staring up at her fire-singed dresses.

Susan folded down beside me.

"Carolina's with him," I said.

"Who's Carolina?"

I rose and swept Amy into my arms, walking her in tight circles, bouncing her. My mind raced. "I have to go to Whistler and get her."

Susan said, "Ellen, what's wrong with you? Sit down. Give Amy here." She extended her arms but I backed away, clutching Amy for dear life.

Amy wailed.

"I have to get Carolina," I said above Amy's screams. "Frank's—" But I couldn't give it words. Words would make it real. "I have to get to Whistler. I have to go *now*."

"What on earth?"

I shouted at her. "Frank's *hurting* Carolina. He's … *sexually abusing* her."

"Hang on a minute," Susan said.

Amy stopped crying.

"But he's got her overnight!" I dumped Amy down, watched half-seeing as she started to clap.

"Who is Carolina?" Susan repeated.

Brigit walked up the stairs. She said to Susan, "Ellen's older daughter." She took my elbow. "Why do you think he's hurting her?"

I looked around wildly. "I sent her. What's *wrong* with me? I sent her up there. She didn't want to go, but I made her."

Brigit and Susan exchanged a glance.

"Drive me home," I ordered.

"You're not going anywhere," Susan said.

"Yes, I am," I said. I looked at the two of them watching me and burst into tears, wracking sobs that shook my shoulders.

Brigit said, "Frank's got custody."

I stared at her angrily, stopped crying. "*I* have custody."

"De facto custody," she said.

"What the hell is that?"

"It'd be kidnapping if you took her," Brigit said.

"What time is he bringing her back?" Susan asked.

"Tomorrow," I cried. "Not until tomorrow! Noon, I think."

Susan said, "We wait, then."

"Wait?"

"Till he delivers her. Then you take off, talk to her." She looked a question at Brigit, who nodded.

"Brigit, I caught Frank—" I was remembering the time I'd seen Frank masturbating on Carolina, but then I lost my train of thought. My voice was shrill. "Oh, Brigit, he's been doing this all along, hasn't he?"

Susan said, "My mother knew and she didn't do fuck all to help me."

I looked at Susan and blinked.

"Get Ellen home," Brigit said to her. "I'll come over first thing, and we'll figure this out then." She peered at me. "Just stay calm and get some sleep. We'll figure things out in the morning."

But I couldn't sleep. About five I finally fell into a sweaty nightmare where Carolina called, "Mommy, Mommy!" and receded into the distance. My feet and legs were useless. I couldn't run to her. She just got smaller and smaller until, when I startled awake, she was no bigger than a dot in the distance. Flashbacks of my father. A half-seen picture of our tack room and men in card-table chairs in a circle.

Eight, I was eight. I was naked. Dead.

I wanted to scream and never stop screaming.

Memories were puzzle pieces; memories made a photograph of a childhood, fought for room with the horror about Frank. Pieces: the barn, a silo. Pieces: our lab scuttling to the basement each evening, tail tucked between her legs, ten minutes before my father came home from work. Pieces: the razor blades under my mattress. My picked sores.

I lurched up, checked on Amy. My brain was trying to find a path that would allow me to feel and still function. I wandered outside to stare up at the mountains overlooking Vancouver, willing Frank to sleep and not touch Carolina, willing her home. As if, by sheer will, I could keep her whole.

Susan woke at nine. At ten, Brigit arrived with boxes. Susan took charge, full of plans. She didn't want Frank to know her name. "Call me Pat," she instructed. She said she'd take us to her house. She sent Brigit and me to pack, which we did with grim attention, filling boxes with important papers, clothes and toys.

We loaded boxes into Susan's car, then she drove it down the street out of sight.

On the lawn, Brigit squeezed my arm.

"I should have known, Brigit. What kind of mother *am* I?" I could have stopped it years ago, I was thinking, even back when Carolina was a baby. How the hell could it have escaped me, especially while Frank and I lived under the same roof?

"Carolina's lucky," Brigit said.

"I might be wrong," I said. Susan was striding up the street towards us. "What if I'm wrong?"

"What's lost?" Susan asked as she reached us, taking my arm. "So what? You're gone a day or two and then you're back."

When we went inside, Amy was awake and crying. I bathed, changed and fed her, hardly seeing her. While she was eating, spilling Cheerios with gusto, Laurence telephoned to say he'd be late.

Frank called at one.

Sound normal, I admonished myself, but I heard breathiness in my voice when I asked if everything was all right.

Frank said things were fine, but he was taking Carolina to a matinee of *A Thousand and One Dalmatians* and wouldn't be back till six.

"Six!" Then I added, in a babble, "Laurence is coming and I wanted Carolina home. She has to *be* here, Frank. It's really *important* to me that she's here."

Brigit made a warning motion.

"Don't be late," I finally said. "All right, Frank? Please, don't be late."

When I hung up, my face was wet with tears. I was shaking inside; I could feel quivers in my legs. "He knows. He knows I know. He's keeping her."

Brigit held me, patted my back. "He doesn't know a thing. How could he? No, no, he doesn't know. He's not keeping her. He's bringing her back."

I pulled away and swiped at my eyes. I looked at Brigit, remembered the fire. "How are *you*?"

She shrugged. "I don't think it's hit me."

"I'm sorry," I said. "I'm not much help, am I?"

"No," she said with a strained grin, "but I don't mind."

"Are you okay to see Laurence?"

Brigit didn't respond, but I supposed having to face my brother wouldn't be easy. "I didn't even stop to think how awkward this could be."

"It wasn't a bad split," Brigit reminded me. "There aren't hard feelings."

I thought about Brigit's pregnancy. I hadn't told Laurence. At least there was that, that I hadn't gossipped.

She asked sharply, "He's not bringing his girlfriend?"

"Marlise? No, he didn't say so. I think he's coming in for business. He said he wanted to stay a couple of days."

"Well, I'll manage. I'll be fine," Brigit said resolutely.

"Thanks," I said and kissed her soft cheek. "Because I really need you here."

"I don't mind. Really."

Laurence and Brigit found an hour's conversation about mutual friends and Laurence's business and Brigit's schooling, but eventually they ran out of things to say. I filled in with falsely cheerful questions, but the tension got worse and worse. Laurence, confused, kept asking what was going on. We assured him nothing was and watched the clock. Four o'clock, it said at last. Five. Five-thirty.

I thought I'd go out of my skin. Brigit and I tried to remember to call Susan "Pat." We kept saying SusanPat or SuePat.

When I heard Frank's key, the key I'd given him after my landlord let him in, I ran across the basement. I fell to my knees at the sight of Carolina. Pink sundress and thongs. Cascades of black hair. I held her and breathed her in. Out of the corner of my eye, I watched Frank. I stood up carefully. He looked usual, normal. I smiled gingerly at him and picked up Carolina.

Brigit lifted Amy. We let Frank get in and drop his parcels, go past us to say hello to Laurence. Then we appeared at the living room door. I said, "We're off."

"Off?"

Laurence raised his eyebrows.

"A women's dance," Brigit said breezily, "with dinner. We're already late."

Frank frowned. "We can keep the kids."

"No," I said quickly.

"No," Susan echoed in her no-nonsense voice, "kids are welcome."

"Carolina," I said, "where's your blanket?" I felt a stab of panic and heard it echo in my voice.

Frank explained that she'd left it on the mountain.

"We'll be home by ten," I said. "Just … uh … make yourselves comfortable."

"Bye now!" Brigit called cheerfully.

"Weren't we going to barbecue?" I heard Frank, bewildered, call.

Outside, Susan walked swiftly down the block and out of sight. I shoved Carolina into my car. Brigit plunked Amy in her car seat. When we straightened, Laurence and Frank were standing behind us. I jumped.

Frank was quiet. Finally, slowly, he asked, "Am I ever going to see you again?"

There was a moment of ghastly silence.

"Don't be silly, Frank." I walked around the car and slid in, slamming my door. My hands were shaking. I watched Brigit start up her van.

I waved and pulled out. In the rearview mirror I watched Laurence and Frank stare after us. Frank had his hands on his hips. Laurence's arms were crossed over his chest. Two blocks ahead, I saw Susan's car move out into the street. Crossing my fingers over the steering wheel—Frank could still jump into his truck—I followed her. I kept checking my rearview.

When we were partway through the city, I asked Carolina about her blanket. "Did you forget Blankie, honey?"

"Daddy said it was too heavy to carry down the mountain."

"Too heavy?" I squawked. Frank *must* have known, I thought. I thought of the hours ahead, Carolina making do without it; it made me furious at him and even more scared.

Beside me, Amy cried. Usually I put a blanket in the side window to block the sun. I followed Susan, who wove in and out of traffic. I concentrated on keeping her in sight.

"I used to have a different daddy," I heard a two-year-old Carolina say. Was that when he began hurting her? Or was that when it got worse?

Susan pulled into the parking lot of an apartment complex. She showed me a locker on the bottom floor where I could stash my things. I kept only the clothes we'd need for tomorrow, Amy's formula, crackers and cereal for Carolina, and Kraft Dinner. I was still shaking when I knocked on Susan's door.

Amy clung to me, peering out at Susan from the safety of my shoulder. I perched on the mattress and box springs Susan used as a sofa; Carolina sat cross-legged by my feet, holding my legs. Susan's place was miles away from being child-proof. She had gewgaws everywhere, little stone dolls, a stereo with tantalizing buttons on a low shelf. Sheer green curtains I could imagine held in grubby fingers.

Susan passed me a cup of tea and tuned the TV to a Disney movie. It distracted Carolina, and even Amy peeked. Susan carefully lowered herself into a recliner and her expression grew dark. Her back hurt, she said.

I watched her. She was pale. "This is a lot, what you're doing for us."

"I wish I was doing better myself," Susan said, sighing deeply. Narrowing her eyes, she peered at the girls. "I guess they have to eat?"

"Oh. Yeah. I brought Kraft Dinner." I scrambled up.

"I'll let you cook it while I call Sandy." She pulled herself up, flinching.

I stopped. "Sandy?"

"My therapist. I want to talk to her about this. I'm not sure what she'll say, besides being pissed off I'm caught in the middle of it."

I ignored my guilt and grabbed Amy up. In the kitchen I sat her on the counter, kept one hand on her thigh, found a pot, started noodles and made up four bottles of formula. I plonked Amy on the floor with some pots and utensils to play with; Carolina was still wrapped up in the TV show. When the Kraft Dinner was ready, I scooped it into three bowls. I loathed the stuff, but I had to eat. Susan had no dining area, so the girls and I sat on the kitchen floor where their mess wouldn't matter. I faltered watching Carolina trying to feed Amy, noodles zooming through the air like planes. I thought, if Frank has touched her… Then, immediately, I didn't believe he had. Carolina was about as tall as doorknobs: how could *anyone?*

Susan called me into the bedroom. I went reluctantly. She said her therapist advised having a bath with Carolina—did Carolina like baths? Yes, I said—and gently telling her what my father had done to me and asking if her father had done the same.

"But—"

Susan rubbed the small of her back. "Every time I get upset this happens." She dug her fingers in.

"I don't need to tell her about me. That's too much for Carolina to hear, Susan," I protested. "She's just little."

"Say it, but say other stuff too. Say it's not her fault. Say you're not angry." She waved her hand.

I nodded, backing down. If it was professional advice …

"I'll look after Amy," Susan finished, turning to stare out her window.

I cleaned up the kitchen, plucking stray orange noodles from the floor. "You want to have a bath with Mommy?" I asked Carolina. We didn't have a bathtub at our apartment, so I expected my offer would sound like a treat.

Carolina was enthusiastic. I bundled her, with her pyjamas, into Susan's small, green bathroom. We used some bubble bath. I blew soap bubbles. After about five minutes, I took my daughter's hand. "Round and round the garden," I began, tracing circles on her little palm, "goes the little teddy bear."

Moving up her arm, I continued, "One step, two steps, tickle you under there! Three steps, four steps"—tangling my fingers—"how'd that bear get in your hair?" Carolina laughed and squirmed.

"Honey, I need to ask you something," I said faintly. I crossed my arms over my chest.

Carolina dunked a yellow plastic duck. She made quacking noises. Her hair was wet at the ends and had lost its curl. It clung to her small upper body, where I could see her ribs through her skin.

"Look at me, Carolina. Mommy needs your attention."

Carolina glanced up.

"When I was a little girl, Carolina," I said, sucking in breath and hoping for the best, though I didn't know what the best would be, "when I was about your size, my daddy made me—uh—touch his penis."

Carolina frowned, shot me a sharp glance and looked down at the duck, pushing it underwater and letting it bounce up through the bubbles. "Why?"

Why? I didn't know why.

Carolina scrambled from the tub and yanked one of Susan's towels from a rod. "I'm not going to be your friend if you talk about this, Mommy. I want Blankie."

Blankie, I thought desperately. "Do *you* ever touch your daddy's penis, Carolina?"

"Of course," she said irritably, facing away from me. "I tickle it, too."

I felt like I'd been slapped. In a minute, I continued neutrally. "My daddy's got big and hard. Does your daddy's?"

"Of course," Carolina said and turned to look at me as if I was being stupid. "All men's do."

"I want you to tell me if Daddy wants you to touch his penis or if he kisses your private parts or wants you to kiss his penis."

"Yuck," Carolina said. She padded towards me. "Can I have a yellow ducky?" She fished Susan's out of the water. "About Father's Day. I can only talk about it before Father's Day."

Father's Day? Frank had had both girls at the mountain on Father's Day.

"I would only whisper it in a secret voice when no one else was here. There's other people here now. Daddy would get mad. All those kinds of daddies and kids can't tell anyone."

"I wouldn't get mad," I said gently.

"No, only Daddy will," said Carolina, with a look of concentration on her small face so intense it was frightening. "I want to go out of this bathroom now." She tried her luck with the doorknob, but her hands were slippery. "I want to see Amy. I told you two times."

"What did you tell me two times, Carolina?" I asked cautiously.

"Why did your daddy hurt you? Because you were split up?" Fear flickered in Carolina's eyes. "I'm scared. You're scaring me."

Oh God, I thought. Mildly, I smiled and said, "Why don't you go out and see Amy then? I'll stay in here for a few minutes."

"I can't get the door open," Carolina said, doubtful I'd let her go.

I got out, dried her and dressed her in pyjamas. I hugged her and told her I loved her. "Go on," I said, opening the door and patting her butt. "Out you go."

I ran hot water. I dunked a washcloth and covered my face. I couldn't make what Carolina had said stay inside my head. I slipped under the water.

Susan knocked. When I didn't answer, she came in anyway. I surfaced. She sat on the toilet. I took one look at her and burst into tears. She'd brought in paper, blue and pink sheets, and she asked me to tell her what had happened, word for word.

"I said everything wrong. I scared her, Susan."

"Wait," Susan broke in. "Carolina's singing." She swung open the door so we could hear.

"Snow's going to get you," Carolina sang liltingly. "Snow is all around you. You need to say gibbidy, gobbedy, goo to make it not get you. Oh, yes, you do. Yes, yes, you do."

Susan wrote it down, closed the door and waited. Obediently, I told her what Carolina had said, my voice bereft of expression.

"What do you think?" I asked when I was through.

"I think it's creepy," said Susan. "'Before Father's Day,' what's that? Something worse happened on Father's Day? I'll bet he used Father's Day to do something he'd never done before. 'C'mon, Carolina, it's Father's Day . . . '"

My stomach was queasy. "And," I interrupted, "she asked did *my* father hurt me because I was split up? Something got a lot worse for her when Frank and I broke up, Susan."

"'All those kinds of daddies and kids can't tell anyone,'" repeated Susan.

"All men's do," I said, sliding down in the tub, submerging. Carolina's statements were awful. I'd wanted her to say no, no, Mommy, that's ridiculous, your overactive imagination, Mommy. I came up, breaking the water. "I wanted her to tell me I was full of shit."

Thoughtfully, Susan said, "You're not, I don't think."

"Carolina's a *baby*. How could terrorizing a child give someone pleasure?" What about her ghosts and witches? Frank knew about them. What about her plastic persona? The withdrawn one? What idiot could miss that sex with a child would be devastating?

"You have to find out more. Tomorrow you can ask her again."

"Ask her *more*, Susan?" I saw her set mouth, her resolute eyes.

Susan laid her hands on her knees. The pink and blue sheets were loose all over the floor, corners of them wet from Carolina's drips. She said, "Yes. Absolutely."

My head was pounding. I looked away from Susan, ignoring her, and eventually she left the bathroom, taking the papers with her.

When I got out the water was cold. I knew I should want to hold and soothe the girls—they were breaking into battles out there, something new since Amy now walked and could grab

Carolina's toys away—but I didn't even want to see them. In the mirror above Susan's sink, I looked haunted. My eyes, always deep-set, had bruisy circles beneath them.

Amy toddled in and let go a long, self-interested speech with all the inflections of English—the stops, the pauses, the emphases—of which I understood not a syllable.

I listened carefully, nodding and frowning where it seemed appropriate.

"I did not!" Carolina yelled. "Amy's lying."

"Did you understand that?" I called. I carried Amy out.

"She thinks I hit her, but I didn't."

Amy wasn't rubbing her arm or anything that indicated she'd been hit. She wasn't crying. "Did you hit her?"

"Mom, she grabbed my sticker. Susan gave me a sticker, see?" Carolina held up a bluebird. "It's mine."

"You don't hit your sister," I said by rote.

It was past their bedtimes. Susan was sequestered in her room, so I guessed I'd share the couch with Carolina and put Amy on the floor where rolling wasn't dangerous. I changed Amy's diaper and got her into sleepers, then coaxed both girls to lie down. Carolina whispered that she wanted Blankie. Amy clutched her elephant. I sang little songs. I drew pictures on Carolina's back. "Apple," she guessed. "Big Bird." I drew randomly on Amy's back.

Susan came out and said, "You can use the bedroom, Ellen. I'm going to stay with friends." She sounded mad. The kids scrambled up.

"You're sure?"

She nodded. "I'll be back about noon. Two at the latest. I'll call Brigit, so you don't have to."

I didn't want to put Susan—a woman Brigit had told me was teetering on the edge—out of her house, but I didn't have anywhere else to go. I got up to hug her, but she was stiff in my arms and I quickly backed away.

"Just get through the night," she said coolly. "Try and keep them from touching stuff."

As soon as Susan left, Carolina started to cry. Maybe she thought Susan was a sort of buffer between us; with Susan around, I wouldn't probe. Amy nodded off but woke, screaming, within minutes. Carolina threw a yo-yo at the wall. "Damn it," I yelled, hating myself for getting angry, carrying her into Susan's room. "Now get into bed and stay in bed, Carolina. I mean it. It's time for sleeping." I dumped her down and left her.

From the living room, in the pauses between Amy's shrieks, I heard Carolina sobbing. I sat cradling my head in my hands.

I spent the rest of the evening going back and forth between children. Carolina chanted, "Black stain one. Black stain two. Black stain in a pot with you." Amy kept falling asleep and jerking awake. She cried intermittently past midnight. Finally I nodded off holding her on the couch and woke at three with a crick in my neck. Gently, gingerly, I carried Amy to the bedroom. Then I sat in a chair at Susan's desk, watching my daughters sleep. I wasn't thinking anything, not really, just watching in the quiet, as if watching might somehow save them.

10

I WAS CRANKY and tired in the morning, and I still had a headache. I fed the girls and sat numbly while Carolina watched "Sesame Street."

Finally I pulled her onto my lap. I tried to make my voice sound unconcerned, but I could hardly look at her. I forced myself to wade in. "What does Daddy do when you touch his penis, Carolina?"

She looked up at me. "He says 'Don't.' Then he does something that I don't like, that hurts me."

"Oh," I said, alarm prickling my skin, "what's that?" Beside me was paper and a pen. I started scratching down what Carolina said.

"I told you. He says 'Don't.'"

"Does he always say 'Don't'?"

"No, sometimes he likes it, when I don't tickle. I don't want to talk about it. It's not very fun." Carolina slid off my lap and played pattycake with Amy.

Later, I asked again. "You'd tell me if Daddy touched your private parts, wouldn't you, Carolina?"

"No," said Carolina firmly.

"Why not, honey?"

"Because it's a secret."

"A secret between you and Daddy?"

"Right. Because there's no lady around. A daddy mouse is a giant rat. A mommy mouse is a giant rat." Carolina seemed mad, but grinned at me. "Just kidding." Then she sat and peered off into nothing, looking unutterably miserable.

"You look sad, Carolina."

Her eyes flashed fear. "No, I don't! My face stays the same no matter what! I'm not upset. I'm not! I'm just not feeling well 'cause of Blankie."

"Yeah," I said, wondering what Frank was *doing* with Carolina's blanket. "Maybe we could go to a store and get a new one."

"No," said Carolina, sighing, "it's okay. Blankie doesn't want to be with me right now anyway. She wants to be with Teddy." Teddy was a stuffed bear at the mountain.

"If your dad hurts you, Carolina, we can stop him."

"Why?"

"Because we don't want you to be hurt any more."

Carolina sighed again and shook her head. Her voice was full of suppressed emotion. "He's been hurting me a couple of times up there."

"How, sweetheart?"

"It hurts with his penis." She sat thoughtfully for a minute, then jumped to her feet. "Why are you writing this down? Because you're a bad girl or something?"

"I'm not going to let anyone hurt you ever again."

"Why?" asked Carolina. "I like him to hurt me. He's my joiner. I didn't want him to hurt me but he still did. I was mad at you 'cause you weren't there."

"I'm here now, Mommy's here. I'm going to keep you safe."

"But it has to be a secret. I just told you a bit. I don't like this. I want to go home."

"It can't be a secret if we're going to stop you from being hurt, Carolina."

"It *is* a secret! I'm not going to tell anybody. I'm scared, you know."

"Oh, I know," I said. "I know you're scared. But you're safe now, pumpkin. Mommy will keep you safe. Can I give you a cuddle?"

"No!"

"We can stop talking about it now," I promised.

"Cut up one," Carolina intoned. "Cut up two. Cut up in a pot with you!"

Susan arrived, and after I'd recounted my conversations with Carolina, she whistled. Then she demanded I report it to a social worker.

I shook my head.

"What did you think was going to happen, Ellen?" Susan's voice was starchy.

"I didn't think." I hadn't thought past talking to Carolina. I thought about how Susan, all through this, had kept pushing me. I wondered whether her own history was interfering, then pushed that ungenerous thought away.

"'It hurts with his penis'?" Susan asked. "That's a pretty definite statement, Ellen. You have to report it."

Again, I shook my head.

"You need somewhere to go, for one thing. And Carolina, she'll need things. Like therapy, for instance. Can you pay for therapy?"

"No," I said guiltily. I searched Susan's face for a sign of benevolence.

Susan took my hands and joined them together, holding them. "If you don't want Frank to take these kids from you, Ellen, then you have to report. *You* can't keep them safe. Incest is a crime. It's the law that you report it."

"Leave me alone," I said, my throat constricted. I pulled my hands free. "I need some time."

"You don't have any," said Susan. She pulled a slip of paper from her jeans. "Here's the number. You report or I report. If I report, it'll look like you're not co-operating. Your choice."

"Wait," I said. "Okay, I'll do it. But I need a few minutes, Susan."

"You've got twenty," she said. She stalked from the room.

My brain raced with old and new images of Frank. When the

old, normal image threatened to block out the new one, I forced myself to remember what Carolina had told me. I was hyperalert. Was I strong enough to fight him? With Carolina as my weapon? A four-year-old?

Would Frank admit it? Because as sure as the sky was blue he wasn't getting anywhere near Carolina unless he admitted it and got help.

The anger was what I needed to steel my nerves. Slowly, I dialled.

"Ministry of Human Resources," I heard.

"I want to speak to a social worker." I *don't* want to speak to a social worker, I thought.

"One moment."

My hand was shakily reaching out to disconnect when I heard a voice say, "Sally March."

I said, "I guess I … I'm calling to report a case of … child sexual abuse."

I could hear the woman coming to attention. Name, please. Address. Victim?

"My daughter," I whispered, gripping Susan's bedspread. "My little girl."

"And what makes you think she was abused?"

"She said so."

"When?"

"Now. Just now. Yesterday and this morning." I was crying again and I yanked tissues from a box by Susan's bed.

"She told you?"

"I asked her."

I heard a trace of surprise. "You asked her?"

"Yes."

"But how did you know she was being abused?"

How did I know she was being abused? I shook my head. "I guessed."

"You *guessed*?"

I rattled on quickly. "I was abused as a child and I remembered it and then it came to me that Carolina was too." I tried to explain some of her symptoms over the years, but I sounded weak, uncertain. I read from my notes.

"And you think the perpetrator was her father?"

"She *said* it was her father." I ought to have lied, I thought, told her that Carolina had come to me instead of me going to Carolina. "Anyway, he's the only man who's had any contact with her."

There was a lengthy pause. "Where are you?"

"I'm at a friend's house. I can't go home. Frank has a key."

"Are you saying he's violent?"

"No," I said, "well, no, but I'm scared to go back there. I'm scared he'll do something if he knows I know." I *was* scared, too, more than I could communicate.

"I can find you somewhere to go. I'll call you back, Ellen. You'll stay by the phone?"

I agreed to.

I threw myself down in Susan's mussed bed. Vaguely I noticed the mess the kids had made; I hadn't lifted a finger to straighten it. But I pulled a pillow over my head. I couldn't stop feeling; I couldn't stop thinking.

Susan came in and sat beside me.

"You did the right thing, Ellen."

"She's calling back," I said, dazed.

"Good," Susan said, nodding again, "good. Good for you."

I watched her leave the room, then pulled the pillow back over my head.

I unstrapped Amy. Her cheeks were cherry red. Carolina undid her seat belt and, tipping her booster seat, spilled forward. I grabbed her hand. I stared up at a red brick house, noticed the pulled drapes. I checked the address Sally had given me. This was it—a transition house for battered women. I took a deep breath. Frank and I had lived together, and Amy had been born, about two blocks away. I carried Amy and our bags up the cement steps and rang the doorbell. Carolina hung back behind my legs. Soon a woman opened a wrought-iron lookout window.

"What's your name?"

I told her.

"We're expecting you," she said. I heard locks, plenty of locks, springing free.

She led me into a living room full of mismatched, stained and torn furniture. There was a stagnant, convalescent smell. "I'm Marie," she said.

I juggled bags and Amy to shake her hand.

"You must be Carolina," she said.

Carolina clutched my pants.

"And Amy," said Marie. Amy, at the sound of her name, hid her head.

"Everyone's upstairs having dinner. Have you eaten? C'mon, I'll show you to your room."

She led us up steps to a dark room at the end of a hall. It was stark. Just beige walls and two single beds with green bedspreads, a battered dresser. "We're not full," Marie said, "so you can have the room to yourselves."

"Do you have a crib?"

"They're all in use. Sorry."

I swung the bags down and deposited Amy on the closest bed. She started to cry. I picked her up again.

"I'll show you around," Marie said. "Unless you'd rather eat first."

Carolina said, "Mom, I'm hungry."

"We'd like to eat, I think." I pulled my mostly empty can of powdered formula and a couple of bottles out and followed Marie up another flight of stairs to the dining room.

The room was noisy with women and children. There was an enormous, dormitory-style table, lots of in-use highchairs. People hardly noticed us.

"Everybody, this is Ellen," Marie said above the din. "And Carolina. The baby's name is Amy."

A couple of women raised hands and said hi. One smiled under a bruised right eye. Marie took us into the kitchen. She showed me a list where women could place grocery orders;

I wrote down Amy's formula and breakfast cereal for Carolina. "Could I make us some sandwiches?"

"They pretty well cleaned out what Renjit made for dinner," Marie said, lifting a pot lid. "So, yeah, help yourself to anything. You should find peanut butter and stuff. When you're finished, come down to the office. It's just across from the door you came in."

Carolina was peeking at roughhousing kids. I made up formula for Amy and found cheese for sandwiches. When we got to the table just one woman was left. She was willowy and pretty.

"What happened to you?" she asked.

"Uh," I said. I busied myself lowering Amy into a highchair.

"Mine broke my damn arm." She lifted her cast, covered with kids' drawings, silly faces and squiggles.

"I… Carolina, you sit here and eat your sandwich. I'll see if there's any milk." I left and got her a cup.

"I'm Nancy," said the woman. "I'm on dish detail." She lit a cigarette and blew smoke. "You need to talk about what happened, honey. It does you a world of good. This is my third time here because I keep going back." She let out a whistly sigh. "It gets to seeming better than the alternative, me and three kids in some roach-filled basement, always looking over my shoulder. I keep thinking at least when I'm with him I know what's coming."

I bit into my sandwich. Carolina didn't seem to be paying us any mind. She was too interested in some bigger boys playing behind the table. Amy was contentedly drinking. "He hurt my daughter," I said under my breath.

Nancy's eyes widened. She glanced around to make sure no kids were listening.

Saying it out loud made it more real. I added, "Sexually."

"Boy, if I ever found out my husband touched any of mine, he'd be dead." She paused.

"I didn't have anywhere to go," I said. "They said to come here."

"Look, sugar, this is a safe house, so at least you can relax and figure stuff out without worrying about him. No men allowed."

I nodded.

Carolina said, "No men? Daddy can't come here?"

Nancy said, "Your daddy doesn't know where this house is. You're safe here."

"No men?"

"That's right," Nancy said.

I said, "Eat your supper, Carolina."

Nancy turned to me. "I'm lucky. You should see some of the women who come in here. Whoo-ee! We got one who was in the hospital first for two months."

Carolina and I were both finished our sandwiches and Amy her bottle. I got up to take our plates to the kitchen, but Nancy stopped me. "I'm on slave duty. You go ahead. They'll have you cooking and cleaning soon enough."

"Thanks," I said.

Nancy butted her cigarette. "You wouldn't think a gal could get lonely. But I'm here to say loneliness is a big problem." She smiled at Carolina. "You wanna make a picture on my cast?"

Carolina wiggled down from her chair and touched the cast, running her finger over the bumps and pictures.

Nancy knocked on it. "It's hard, eh? It's a big hard bandage on my hurt arm." Nancy rapped on the cast again, encouraging Carolina to do the same. "Honey, tomorrow you get some pens from your mama and I'll let you do a picture on it. You think about what you want to draw, like Daffy Duck. Okay? Is it a date?"

Carolina looked at me. When I nodded, she said, "Big Bird."

"Big Bird it is," Nancy concurred.

I took the kids down to the office. It was like any office anywhere, a jumble of desks and paper. Marie waved me to a chair. "Got your sea legs?"

"Nancy has a hard bandage and I get to draw Big Bird," Carolina announced.

"A cast," I corrected. "Her bandage is called a cast."

"Because her arm got hurt," said Carolina. "She got an owwy." She frowned. "There are big boys up there."

"There are lots of kids here," said Marie, nodding. "Come on and I'll show you our playroom."

We followed her to a basement playroom that seemed well, if scrappily, appointed. Carolina went across to an easel. "My daddy," she stated deliberately, "can come here if he wants."

Marie said, "Oh, no, he can't, Carolina. There's no men allowed." She walked across and showed Carolina a list of house rules. "See? See Number One rule? That says, 'No men allowed.'"

"I don't care anyway," said Carolina, radiating fear. "He might be outside that window with a gun, you know."

"No, he's not."

"You couldn't stop him," Carolina said.

"Oh, yes, I could. This is a house where women are strong, Carolina."

She peered up at Marie skeptically.

"I'd like to get these girls to bed," I said.

Back in our room, I wished there were two of me. If the balance of my attention swung to Carolina, Amy cried. If the balance swung to Amy, Carolina begged for another story. I went between beds, knowing I was doing neither girl much good.

Eventually they slept. I heaped blankets and pillows around Amy like crib sides and, leaving the door open, went down the hall to the office. In another room I heard a woman singing a lullaby in a language I didn't understand. Further on, I heard cross words in English.

Marie had me answer questions she read from a six-page intake sheet. They were not, on the whole, questions pertinent to our situation. I did a lot of shaking my head.

"I have to say, Ellen, that we're out of our league here. It's fair to let you know that. We've never had a sexually abused child at this transition house."

I nodded, though I felt violated after her probing. I just wanted to go home.

"We advise our residents to get lawyers, and you should do that too, to fight for custody."

"Frank doesn't want custody," I said quickly. "He never wanted it."

"Access, then. Visitation. Are you on welfare?"

"No," I said. "UI."

"You'll have to apply for welfare. You're not eligible for UI unless you're looking for a job. You have a month here if you want it. We never advise reconciliation."

"No," I said, "there won't be a reconciliation. We were separated before I found out about ... about this." I paused. "Is there child care here?"

Amy began to cry in the distance.

"There's the child care room, but that's only open for four hours a day. And it's not for babies."

"I'll need a homemaker, then," I said. "I can't take Carolina back to daycare."

"We don't allow homemakers."

I looked at her.

"Transition house doesn't allow women to have homemakers."

"But I need help." I was holding back tears, anxious to get to Amy in case she'd rolled to the side of the bed. I wiped my palms on my jeans, sliding to the edge of my chair.

"Women learn parenting skills here; it's a part of what we do." She paused and looked severely at me. "We don't allow spanking."

"I have to go to Amy," I said, rising, but I stopped at the door. "What's discipline got to do with getting homemakers?"

"Child care takes women's minds off their problems," Marie said.

I opened my mouth, but hearing Amy I shook my head and ran down the hall.

She was still restrained by the pillows. But she was in full convulsion, terror slicking her eyes, her head thrashing. I automatically started soothing her. "Amy, it's Mommy. Mommy's right beside you, sweetheart." My nerves were on fire and I wasn't thinking. I tried to put Amy's soother into her mouth without putting it in her hand first. As she gagged and flailed violently to escape it, I finally understood.

I backed away from the bed, a hand clapped over my mouth.

Frank was the reason for Amy's night terrors. Frank was why I couldn't spoon-feed her. Why she'd sailed off my breast.

I slammed my hands over my ears. I was scared to go near her. I slid down, small sounds escaping my mouth.

I didn't hear a knock, but suddenly Marie was beside me, bending to me, holding me. Harrowing sobs wracked my body.

11

AS CAROLINA WAS dressing the next morning, she said, "My ears are getting better."

"Oh," I said, "were they hurting?"

"Yeah, a lot."

"Popping from going up and down the mountain?"

"Yeah, forever." She pulled on yellow shorts and a striped green T-shirt.

Like everything else Carolina said that seemed vaguely relevant, I wrote it down. In the last few months I'd gone back to keeping the journal I'd written in only sporadically over the years.

Amy was in a good mood. She was padding around in her sleepers, giggling as I tried to catch her to change and dress her. I thought of my night's fear—that I didn't know how to be her mother, that I was frightened of doing the wrong thing as a parent, frightened even to go near her, to touch her—and shook my head. As I caught her, as I lay her on her back to change her, trying to hold her down while I snapped snaps fast, I found myself watching her mouth.

Amy, Amy, sitting in a tree,
k-i-s-s-i-n-g.
First comes Dad and says it's a bottle:
Come, little baby, let's have a cuddle.

Somehow I had to keep an eye on two traumatized little girls and at the same time arrange for welfare, for a lawyer. I had to talk to the social worker. I had to arrange—the end of the month was fast upon us—to get all my belongings moved out of my apartment. Into storage? Certainly I couldn't take the new apartment, with Frank knowing where it was.

Finally, I got us to the kitchen, where I gave Carolina cereal and Amy a bottle. I found a small bowl of berries for Carolina. Just as she was finishing them, Nancy appeared.

"Those berries made Michael—he's my middle kid—sick, Ellen. I was just coming to throw them out."

Carolina said, "Big Bird!"

I said, "Carolina, you'll have to tell me if you get a tummy ache. Put your dishes in the sink."

"If I get a tummy ache you'll take me to the doctor, Mommy. So I can't tell you, really."

I let this sink in, then turned to Nancy. "Where is everyone?"

"Downstairs, vying for the phone."

"I need to use it."

"Good luck. Anyway, staff asked me to tell you to come to the office."

Two new workers asked me to repeat the story I'd told Marie the previous evening. They seemed uneasy, glancing often at each other, and one of them made furious notes as I spoke.

"Can I read that?" I pointed to the notebook. I felt stripped of dignity, repeating this story over and over, having it—and impressions of me—recorded.

The workers looked at each other, didn't answer.

"We'll have to bring it up at a staff meeting," one said at last. Amy had her fists tangled in my hair. "Theoretically, I suppose so. But no one's ever asked before."

There was a constant line-up to use the phone. I tried to occupy Amy and Carolina while I waited. I suggested Carolina go down to the playroom, but she wasn't confident enough, considering the "big boys."

After hanging around for nearly an hour, I asked Carolina to give me a hug.

"No hugs," she said, working to piece together an adult puzzle. "They're in the hospital getting fixed."

Every time Carolina opened her mouth, what she said hurt me. I assumed what I hoped was a benign expression. "What time will they be getting home?" I asked.

"At nine-thirty. But then they're going into my belly to be babies. They're very scared to come out. They might get hurt. Or they might hurt someone."

I felt a wave of heartbreak. "C'mere, Carolina."

She shook her head.

"I love you," I said.

Tonelessly, she replied, "I love you, too."

Finally I got to the phone. Women were still waiting, so I confined my calls to business. The first was to my friend Simone. I explained our situation and asked if she could get a crew of her housemates together to clear out my apartment.

She sounded exasperated. "Frank's not going to hurt you. Why do you think he'll hurt you?"

"Simone, I don't know. All I know is that I'm in this transition house and I can't move my stuff. I can't afford to hire movers. We're in trouble here."

"We can have a house meeting and discuss it, I guess."

Amy was crying. I set her on my hip and tried to concentrate on talking to Simone. "Please," I begged.

"The idea is to move your stuff into storage?"

"Yes."

"You're giving up the apartment? Are you sure you should do that?"

"Simone, ask me my name. I don't even know *that*. Can you help me?"

When I hung up, I felt defeated. But I kept dialling.

To get a lawyer I was told I had to appear at the legal aid office in person.

To get welfare I was told I had to appear at the district office in person. I asked to speak to Sally March, the social worker I'd talked to before, and when I was transferred through, Sally told me she'd been assigned to our case.

Case? I thought. We're a case now?

Sally said Carolina would be interviewed by a specially trained social worker from the child abuse team. And by a police officer. And that Carolina would need to be seen by a doctor.

"A doctor?" I asked, puzzled and alarmed.

"Someone who can tell if she's been injured."

I was stunned. Injured? She hadn't been injured. I'd *know* if she had been injured.

"Amy too?" I rambled on about Amy, about Amy's convulsions and her refusal to eat, her dark under-eye bags, her fear of accepting soothers or bottles, how she flew off my breast while she was nursing, how I was scared Frank was going to hurt us and just scared, period, and how my own memories came hot and heavy and, and, and …

"Have you slept, Ellen?"

I admitted I hadn't. I'd been awake all night.

"Eaten?"

"Not much."

"You won't do those girls much good if you don't take care of yourself."

"No, I know, I realize that," I said.

"Can I ask you something?"

I made a small noise of assent.

"I'm pretty new at this, and I'd like to give you the benefit of the doubt, but Ellen, is this … a ploy? To get back at the children's father?"

Amy and Carolina were fighting. "Get back at Frank for what? I don't know what you mean."

"Well, moms sometimes claim abuse when they want their husbands not to have contact with them."

"That's preposterous." I rubbed my neck. "What a stupid thing to think."

"Do you … can I ask how you feel about men?"

"What do you mean?" I asked thinly.

"Are you a feminist? Do you … hate men, Ellen?"

"What's one thing got to do with the other?" I squeaked.

"Don't get touchy."

I set my teeth. "I don't hate men. I … do … not … hate … men. Have you got that? Is that absolutely clear?" Livid, I dropped the phone into its cradle. Her accusations rolled in me like hot butter.

Do you hate men, Ellen? I heard again, a sort of echo. Do you think Frank had intercourse with the baby? Is that what you *really* think, Ellen? Is it?

After lunch, I packed Carolina and Amy into the car to drive to the appointments I'd made that morning. I was scared and alert; my car, an old rattletrap, was highly visible, and Frank could be hunting for us. I appeared at my appointments shaking. After interminable delays, after I had demeaned myself in a welfare worker's office and been treated carelessly at legal aid, I drove to our new apartment and asked the manager to release me from my tenancy agreement. She was the mother of a daughter a year younger than Carolina and had herself escaped a violent spouse; she tore up our contract.

I decided to hide my car in transition house's back alley.

≈

1965

Mom says pretend I'm Nancy Drew. Mom says if I'm a detective I can out-detective Dad's detectives.

Stupid detectives. Laurence and Margaret and I see them everywhere, men in dark suits.

Climbing down from the hayloft.

In the north field.

On the playground at school.

On the road in cars.

Mom says they're lurking. I love that word, "lurking." I try and lurk too.

≈

As I pulled the car up behind the house, I asked the girls if they wanted to go to Dairy Queen. I'd had enough crisis for today; I was desperate for something bland.

"We better drive, though, Mommy," Carolina shouted when she saw me step out and pocket my keys.

"No, it's really close," I said. I hauled Amy's stroller from the trunk.

"I get to ride in it," said Carolina, jumping out and pulling on my shirt. "Me, me. My turn!"

"You know you're too big, Carolina. You can push it if you want."

"My stomach hurts," complained Carolina as we got underway. She lagged behind. She touched her thighs. "My these hurt. My knees hurt. My feet hurt."

"Don't you want an ice cream?"

"I can't walk, Mommy. It hurts to walk."

"For heaven's sake," I said, exasperated. "All right. You walk on my feet and I'll push Amy." Carolina stepped onto my feet and clutched my legs. It was an innovative, if painful, solution.

Amy would eat ice cream, at least. When we were through I mopped sticky faces and hands as best I could, then we trundled back to transition house in a chorus of Carolina's complaints.

I thought about how often I had heard these complaints of hers; I remembered other trips where she had refused to walk. The social worker's talk about injuries made me consider whether there was a physical cause, and if so, what it might be.

It was chilling, but I wondered, suddenly and for the first time, about penetration. For God's sake, I chastised myself. What had I thought 'It hurts with his penis' meant? But I *hadn't* thought. I had layer upon layer of illusion; each layer was like a shield, protecting me from the one below it. I only had the ability to strip away a little at a time.

I bathed and changed Amy, then put her down for a late nap. I sat Carolina down for a talk. Over and over, realizing I'd barely covered this territory at Susan's, I told her what had happened with her father wasn't her fault. She insisted it was. I told her she'd been very brave to tell me and said that I, with my father, had never told.

"Why?" Carolina licked her lips. "*Why?*"

"Because I thought what my father did was supposed to happen. I thought it happened because I was a bad girl. But I wasn't. My dad was a bad dad. It's never the little girl's fault, Carolina."

"I only told you a little bit."

"Sweetie, I know that. So we need to figure out a way that if you want to tell me something, I'll listen. You could say, 'Mom, I need to talk.' Or you could … I don't know … pull on my clothes. Or tap me on the leg. Kick me if you have to. And then if there're times you don't want to talk about it and I'm bugging you, you just tell me, 'No, Mommy, I don't want to talk.' Okay?"

"It hurts to poop, Mommy," Carolina said gravely. "And my tummy feels all sloppy."

Oh, God, I thought. "We're making a doctor's appointment for you. She can check you over and make sure you're healthy. I'm sure you're fine." But I wasn't sure any more, not about anything.

Carolina crawled onto my lap and said she missed Blankie. I held her and smoothed her hair.

My mind was racing. Why had I believed Frank had only fondled her? It felt stubborn and dangerous, suddenly, this minimalizing I'd been doing. Frank had orally abused Amy and he had entered Carolina. My head was hot.

May, one of the on-duty workers, swept in to say that Sally March had called about Carolina's doctor's appointment. She passed me a slip of paper. "It's July 27, at 2:00 P.M."

"July 27?" I was faint with anger. "A month from now?"

"Dr. Cole has a regular practice too and she's backed up," May explained as if she were talking to a naughty child.

Carolina tugged at my shirt. "But we can't wait a month!" I said.

May shrugged.

Carolina whispered in my ear. "It's my bummy, Mommy."

I frowned and listened.

"Dad hurt my bummy."

That bowel movement. That bloody poop smeared with strands of white, I thought slowly. With great deliberation, I looked back at May. "I want that appointment by Thursday. If you can't arrange it, I'll arrange it. But it can't wait."

May blinked. I realized it wasn't her fault. But what I'd asked for—a crib, a homemaker, an appointment—was already much less than we needed.

"I mean it," I told her. "It's not negotiable."

≈

1962

Eight men dressed in suits, sitting in a circle. Poker chips. Light, not dark out: afternoon or early evening. I strip off my top and undershirt, my shorts. I move to each of their laps. I know how to suck them; I want to suck them.

Shelves of trophies. Peg boards of ribbons. Saddles and bridles.

≈

By the end of another sleepless, memory-deluged night, I'd convinced myself that I was mad. At 6:00 A.M. I called the Ministry of Human Resources' emergency line and begged for a homemaker.

"Mom," said Carolina at breakfast, unaware of my fragile state of mind, "you choose what I should have. I want what I don't eat at my daddy's."

Amy's old formula was gone. Though the staff had shopped, they'd bought another brand. In slow motion, I prepared it.

Carolina, seated at the table, told Nancy that her son Shawn couldn't touch the bear she clutched. When he did, Carolina cried, "Daddy touched it!" and threw it bouncing across the room. "Close the windows! Close the windows!"

Amy wouldn't eat. She took one suck on her bottle, scrinched up her eyes and started wailing.

It didn't matter how shaky I was—I had to get back into my apartment. Simone and her friends had agreed to move me into storage the next day, and I needed to get our clothes first. I asked if someone from transition house could go with me. But a worker told me their policy was that women could only go back accompanied by police officers. I countered that we could call the mountain and, if Frank was there, a two-hour drive away, we could be in and out before he could possibly arrive. I was going, I said, but I'd appreciate help. I *need* help, I felt like screaming. I was scared of Frank and almost paralyzed by my run of emotions.

"It's against the rules," she told me firmly.

When the emergency homemaker arrived at two, I left the girls in her care and started on my jittery, cross-city drive. At the apartment I found a mountain of kids' clothes I'd been asking Frank to return for weeks, laundered and folded. It was creepy, menacing. I looked through the pile, unsuccessfully, for Carolina's blanket, then jammed the stuff willy-nilly into green garbage bags. I pulled more clothes from hangers. Ten minutes, in and out. I was so nervous I jumped at the rustle of mice.

Back at the shelter, I planned to leave the girls with the homemaker and crawl into bed. But as I was hauling the bags past the office, a worker, Maggie, called out to me, "Carolina has her doctor's appointment in forty-five minutes, Ellen. Be ready in ten."

I yelled okay, knowing I couldn't say I was in no shape to go.

Maggie appeared in the doorway. "When was the last time you had a bath?"

"A bath?" I said. I looked down at myself. I was still in the clothes I'd worn Saturday night. "Right," I said, embarrassed.

We took the transition house station wagon. I ran for Amy's car seat and Carolina's booster, but it took a while to strap them into the wagon because I couldn't get my arms and hands co-ordinated. Maggie complained, "We haven't got time for that." I tried to hurry. I plunked Amy into her seat—she was calm despite having eaten only crackers all day—and told Carolina to climb up. She got in very reluctantly, then started kicking. She kicked the back of the front seat and, at last, punched and kicked me. From the driver's seat, Maggie said, "For God's sake! I thought you wanted this appointment!" I didn't know what to do. That morning I'd told Carolina to kick me if she needed my attention, but not now, not with Maggie mad and us in a big hurry. I spoke to her sharply, belted her in and climbed into the front seat, yanking the door closed.

I looked back at Carolina. Very deliberately she turned her face away from me. I stared out at the passing city streets and felt again the impossibility of doing right by her—what had she been trying to tell me? That Frank had abused her in his truck? I couldn't find a way to articulate this suspicion to Maggie without it sounding histrionic, so I didn't say anything. I pulled on my stringy, wet hair.

Both girls fell asleep on the way, and waking them was a misery. My voice was thin and wavery as I coaxed them up. I passed a fussy Amy to Maggie and lifted a remote and stiff Carolina into my arms.

The doctor, Jamie Cole, wanted to see me first. I left the girls with Maggie and moved towards the office like a zombie.

Dr. Cole was a large, stern woman, and I was instantly intimidated. I sat carefully in the diminutive chair beside her high desk. Idly I noticed a wooden seagull above her examining table, a bird that "flew" if you pulled a string; it was a duplicate of the bird I'd given Frank for his May birthday. He'd hung it in his bedroom, he'd said. I cleared my throat, but I couldn't look into Dr. Cole's eyes.

"Now," she said, "what's the big emergency?"

I was trying to pull a reply from the muck of my brain when a nurse knocked and interrupted. Dr. Cole spoke sharply to her.

Then she turned back to me. A stethoscope wobbled against her chest as she drummed impatient fingers against her thigh. "How did you discover that your daughter was being sexually abused?"

Whatever verbal powers I usually had had evaporated. I offered up what I'd said to others, presenting it in a halting, questioning voice. "I, uh, I ... guessed?"

The doctor rolled her eyes. "Well then, tell me how you could guess something like that." She consulted her notes. "Ellen, is it?"

In a rush I said, "I remembered my own incest and then it came to me that Carolina was being hurt."

"It *came* to you," the doctor slowly repeated, pursing her lips.

"She said it was her bum." It was all I could think of to say. Trying to add something of merit, I went on, "She's had blood in her stool."

"Young children don't know the difference between their bottoms and their vaginas," the doctor said, scratching something down.

I was certain Carolina did. Positive this symptom deserved more attention, I lifted my chin. "I'm worried because of the blood."

The doctor arched her eyebrows. "Was it *through* her stool?"

"Uh, smeared on top, I think," I said, trying to remember. But how the blood looked wasn't something I'd paid attention to. "I asked her to tell me if it happened again, but she started flushing the toilet."

"I see," Dr. Cole said slowly. "And why did you think of sexual abuse?"

I frowned, confused. "I didn't, not then."

"Why *now*?" she pressed.

"Because of how Carolina's always been," I said weakly. I was making a mess of things. I added, "Trouble sleeping. Peeing her bed. Wanting to tie her friends up. Unusual fears. Genital rashes. Refusing to go to her father's." It was impossible at the best of times to encapsulate all my concerns about Carolina in a sentence or two; now it was even harder, because everything I said felt like it was being pulled through glue.

"And what does Carolina say?"

"She says he hurt her." I made it sound tentative.

"Does she indeed?" Dr. Cole tapped a knuckle on her chin and regarded me skeptically. "I'm ready to see her, then, if that's all you have to say. Please go and get her."

I started to get up but stopped myself. I had to ask. "Can you check Amy too? Just so I'm sure?"

Dr. Cole cocked her head.

"So I know she's okay?" My voice was faint with pleading.

"You're not implying that there's been abuse of your baby?"

"No," I said, "yes. I don't know. I didn't know about Carolina, either, a few days ago."

Dr. Cole didn't reply. Quivering, I got up. As I retrieved Amy, I could feel myself going weird inside, as if I were in a fog and couldn't see. I *could* see, but not properly. The brown-carpeted hall looked like mud to me. My palms were clammy and in my chest there was a buzzing sensation. I could feel my fingertips tingling.

Just get through this, I told myself.

Amy's exam was easy and brief, and as I expected her genitalia were completely normal. I thought of having the doctor check Amy's mouth, too, but I didn't want another of her looks. Like an automaton I went for Carolina.

Carolina was scared. In the chair beside Dr. Cole's desk, she cuddled in against my chest, sucking her thumb. Brusquely Dr. Cole tried to draw her out: "Did your father hurt you?"

Carolina shook her head violently.

"I'll ask you again, Carolina," the doctor repeated with obvious distaste. "*Did* your father hurt you?"

"He only kicked me and hit me," said Carolina in a squeaky, high-pitched voice.

"Draw me a picture of you and your baby sister and your mommy and daddy." The doctor pushed paper and a blue crayon towards Carolina.

Carolina looked up at me. I nodded.

Though she often drew quite unusual pictures of people—figures without torsos, say—now she drew stick figures with all of their parts, a family holding hands.

A part of me was perversely pleased. Instinctively, Carolina knew she had to protect herself.

Dr. Cole wanted to reassure her. "Today is just for talking. I'm not going to examine you today, Carolina."

Carolina slipped fully into her plastic persona. I watched as she climbed off my lap and began, apparently happily, to explore Dr. Cole's office. She touched a pile of speculums on a shelf. Dr. Cole was completely taken in. I didn't know what to say: She's not herself, Dr. Cole? I said nothing, because I wasn't myself, either, and the complexity of this made it impossible to communicate.

Though Carolina's back was turned, Dr. Cole said, "Are you frightened of your father, Carolina?"

"Of course not." Said with disdain.

"Has he touched you in a way you didn't like?"

Carolina turned and shook her head. She did this well, convincingly, with not too much emphasis, as if the doctor were wasting her time with such ridiculous questions. Carolina had more important concerns, she managed to imply.

After another minute of this kind of questioning, Dr. Cole turned to me. "She's obviously comfortable, so I'll go ahead with the exam."

My mouth dropped open. But you can't … you said … you told her you wouldn't, I wanted to say. The words stuck in my throat.

"Come along, Carolina," Dr. Cole ordered briskly.

I helped Carolina take off her clothes and clamber up on the examining table. Dr. Cole didn't offer a gown. Carolina lay back. I stood beside her with sweat running down from my armpits. She smiled in her inaccessible, cardboard way, until her eyes were seized by the bird above the table. Doctor. Daddy. Doctor. Were the two of them mixing hopelessly in her brain? I held her shoulder as Dr. Cole snapped on plastic gloves and arranged materials.

As the doctor probed, Carolina went dead still. When the doctor took a swab, she jerked violently and her eyes widened.

The doctor spoke over her to say I could ignore any further shows of blood. She didn't say why, and I didn't know how to tell her this seemed crazy to me. I just nodded.

"I'd like to see Carolina alone now," said Dr. Cole when she was through. "And then I'd like to talk with Maggie. You can wait outside."

"Mommy," Carolina said in a tinny voice, sitting up and clutching me. She didn't want me to leave her.

I wanted to protest, but I didn't dare. "I'll be just outside," I promised.

I floated down the muddy hall past Amy as if she weren't mine and out the door into the harsh sunlight. I collapsed onto the clinic steps. Frank had not abused the kids? That's what Dr. Cole had implied. I ran through the list of all the things I'd noticed and concluded that the abuse was real. There was no other possibility—onto that I hung tenaciously. I looked at the parked cars as I let a horrible thought form and bully forth: If Frank didn't do it, it must have been me.

I dropped my face in my hands, full of self-loathing. Me? Not Frank?

When Maggie brought the girls out, I couldn't meet her eyes. I had no memory of ever having even a sexual *thought* about my daughters, but while I was sleeping? Sleepwalking? *I* was the monster here?

Partway to the shelter, Maggie said, quite cheerfully, "By the way, Ellen, Carolina's exam was positive for sexual abuse."

I flicked a glance at her and blinked surprise. Carolina's exam was positive? After the doctor had acted like I was making it up? Carolina's exam was positive? Leave me alone, I thought, all of you, just leave me alone. I held myself tight, but I was scarily dizzy.

Brigit arrived after ten that evening. I was glad to see her, but I couldn't find a path out of myself to let her know I cared she'd come. In the deserted kitchen, we made mugs of peppermint tea and carried them back to my room, sitting cross-legged on the floor. The room was dim, lit only by an alley street lamp. Brigit seemed distant in a way I couldn't readily identify. For a while, I watched the sleeping kids. I was used to feeling a kind of mindless devotion to them, but tonight I saw them as a backdrop to Brigit. I desperately wanted to talk to her about what had been going on, but how could I? If I told her how I'd felt accused by the doctor and then turned it on myself, it would just seem ... crazy. I was gravely ashamed of myself for concocting such an explanation in the first place and too shaken to explain that, horrible as it was, blaming myself had been easier than sketching out scenes of Frank's penis entering Amy's mouth or Carolina's vagina.

Talking was like leaping a gully, but finally I surprised myself by wailing, "This is like chasing ghosts. How can I know what's real?"

Brigit murmured in a way that must have been meant to be sympathetic but conveyed only strain.

I was too swept into myself to stop once I'd begun. I noticed I was gesticulating, as if the patterns of my hands and arms allowed a release words alone did not. I rattled on about how hard it was to know exactly what had happened.

Brigit raked her hands through her hair.

"What's bugging you?" I asked, stopping finally.

"What's bothering *you*?" Brigit countered. "You seem ... different."

I struggled for words. "The sadness is so deep, Brigit. There's been, I don't know, a rupture so deep I ... Nothing's what I thought it was. It's not even like there's a wound inside me. It's something worse, deeper ... " I trailed off, picking at a scab on my arm.

There was a lengthy, thick pause.

"Maybe it's trust," I went on. "Maybe it's that I used to believe in people. What was it Anne Frank wrote? That she thought people were basically good at heart? Well, I *don't* think so, not now."

On one of the beds, Carolina shifted. She kicked the sheet off and her nightie slid up, exposing her bottom.

I closed my eyes against the sight. "We had our doctor's appointment today," I said softly. Then I burst out, "Frank should be here! He should be the one going through this, not me." I paused and looked sadly at Brigit. "It was positive."

"The exam?"

"They won't tell me the details," I said. "I get so confused. It's only me standing between these girls and Frank, but all the workers act like I'm ... I don't know ... overreacting? Embellishing?" I made a strangled sound. "Like I'm lying. I've got all the years of worry that suddenly add up, but it doesn't mean anything to them. To them it's as if I fell off Mars."

Brigit nodded, but she didn't say anything.

"I can't even *be* honest, that's the problem. I don't know what Frank did. Like the stuff with my dad, how am I supposed to know what's real?" I hadn't told Brigit or anyone else—I might never—about the memory of group fellatio. It was too outlandish, and too deeply painful. I felt reluctant to go on, so I shook my head and dipped into my brain for a change of subject. "Did you find out about fire insurance yet?"

"The landlady already has a crew in. I'm staying in Tanya's room," Brigit said, her voice measured.

"For you, I meant?"

"Ellen," Brigit said, her eyes rounding with hurt, "don't. You know I didn't have insurance. I lost everything."

Had I known this? I couldn't recall.

"My parents say they'll help, though." She gave a wan smile.

For a good while, neither of us spoke. The room was cool, and I shivered. I understood somewhere in my slow, overpressured brain that something had altered between us while my attention had been diverted, perhaps *because* my attention had been diverted, perhaps because I was all need and my need was striking up against hers, unyieldingly. But it was beyond me, in the shape I was in, to do anything about it.

Eventually Brigit got up to go, and I saw her to the door.

In the morning there was a new group of transition house staff, because the women worked four-day rotations. While I had garnered minimal sympathy from the first round of workers, this second bunch was appalled by the disruption in policy I'd caused and showed it at every opportunity, going suspiciously silent or shooting dirty looks as I passed.

Amy still hadn't eaten even though I'd gotten some of her usual formula. I offered a panoply of foods; when I gave her a bowl of strawberries she stuck her hands in it, steeled her jaw and made grunting noises, squeezing the berries to pulp, but she ate nothing. By midafternoon, she was convulsing and I carried her, screaming, to our room. An hour or so later, she fastened lucid eyes on me and cried, "Oh, Mama! Oh, Lina!" I heard her heartbreak, understood our names and pulled her, shaking, into my arms. She didn't object, though her eyes immediately glazed and the choking and gagging and screaming resumed.

Shouting to be heard over Amy's shrieks, Carolina said, "There are no rules at the mountain, Mommy!" She shoved a piece of paper under my nose. "Write rules for our room."

Holding Amy, I wrote as Carolina dictated.

"No men," Carolina said. "Hugs at bedtime, which is at eight o'clock. Write that."

I complied.

"Stick," Carolina said. "Write stick."

"Why?"

"I can only go out of our room if I have a weapon." She

picked up a toy airplane she'd brought from the transition house basement and held it up like a bat. "Write weapon."

I wrote weapon.

"Daddy will get me if I don't carry a weapon. I can't look out the window."

"You don't have to see your father any more, honey," I promised quietly, unsure that I should.

"I am so. I spend weekends and Wednesdays with him."

"Not any more, Carolina," I said, rocking Amy.

"The skin on your face doesn't peel."

Stop, I thought, shut up.

"I want new skin. The skin on my head won't peel like on my feet. If I cut off my head, I'll get new skin."

I drew in my breath. Jesus, I thought, you poor little girl. Cut off your head? I thought fast. I said, "Honey, everyone's skin gets a little bit new all the time. Probably by later this month, all your skin will be new."

"Probably?"

"Well, for sure by August first," I said. I laid Amy on one of the beds and returned to Carolina, taking her hands in mine.

"August second. I'll have new skin August second." She paused and pulled her hands free. "I want blood."

It was dizzying.

"Like grownup ladies," she added.

"Periods, you mean?"

"Periods make you safe."

I closed my eyes. I was trying hard to keep up. "You're not supposed to have your period, Carolina. Periods are for grown-ups."

"I'll be grownup if I have periods."

"No, honey." Then I said, "You didn't get hurt because you're little, but because your daddy did a bad thing."

"No, he didn't."

"Nobody has a right to hurt you, and that's that."

"My daddy touched me in ways that hurt."

"I'm sorry," I said. "I'm so sorry he did."

"That's okay. I didn't mind." Carolina played with her airplane, zooming it across the uncarpeted floor.

I picked up Amy's bottle in the hope she might accept it.

My attorney, Meara Lindley, a rotund, middle-aged woman I'd found through Brigit, lived on one of the coastal Gulf Islands. She came into the city to talk to me in a colleague's office—I'd left the girls with the homemaker—reviewing the process I'd have to go through to gain custody of Carolina and Amy. Carolina would be interviewed by Roma Flagge, a social worker from the child abuse team Sally March had mentioned. Sometime after that, Frank would be interrogated by the police, and sometime after that, the police would decide on a plan of action. In British Columbia, Meara said, no child younger than six had ever testified on the witness stand.

"The witness stand?" I didn't know what she meant.

"It's highly unlikely Carolina would be found competent to testify, Ellen."

Testify? I looked at Meara like she had spots. "Testify? Carolina can't testify." Fear flooded through me. I remembered how hard it had been to face my father across a courtroom, and I hadn't been describing abuse. "She's too little! I can't do that to her, Meara!"

"There's the question of safety, though."

"Safety?" I liked Meara intuitively, but she was throwing too much at me, too many ideas that I couldn't absorb.

"If Frank is not charged, if there's no court proceeding, then there's no reason to deny Frank access or custody."

I stared at her.

"I'm sorry, Ellen. The facts are, if he's not convicted, he has the legal right to see his children."

"He doesn't!" I looked around wildly, as if there were someone else present to dispute this.

"We'll try to stall him. We'll try to get a custody agreement with no access, open-ended. And when he does get contact, we'll try to make sure it's supervised." She noticed my confusion.

"That means your social worker recommends that a neutral party be present during his visits. Normally, the court will make an order for three or six months. If Frank behaves, then he'll be given open visits. You say he's not interested in custody?"

I nodded. Frank and I had discussed it when we separated.

"Because there's a good chance he'd win it. The courts don't think highly of mothers in your situation. They think mothers accuse their ex-es of abuse just to be spiteful."

This was terrifying news. The courts were no help? They could give my kids to Frank? "But we parted amicably! I'll go underground first. I'll leave Canada."

"Hold on, hold on," she said, reaching for my hand. "You're getting ahead of yourself. Like I said, there's every chance we can stall him. When's Carolina's child abuse interview?"

I shook my head.

"I'll find out and go with you."

"Thanks," I said.

"You've gotten on welfare," Meara said, ticking off points on her fingers. "And legal aid's been approved. And Carolina's been to the doctor. Do you know what the doctor's report was?"

"Only that it was positive."

"I'll find that out, too. Things should move fairly quickly from here. Does Frank have a lawyer?"

I shrugged.

"He will if he's not an absolute fool. It makes the police far less willing to arrest. Unless I'm vastly mistaken, there won't be charges. Between lack of witnesses, Carolina's age and your reluctance to have her testify . . . "

I said, "I'm scared," and my eyes filled with tears.

"I'll do my best for you, Ellen."

I nodded. Meara was a very warm woman, and I felt comforted.

"In the meantime, button your lip. No contact with Frank"—how did she know I fought occasional urges to call him, meet him and warn him?—"or with any of your mutual friends. Or his family. The less said the better."

After seeing Meara, I picked up the kids and drove to Simone's. From my welfare cheque, I reimbursed her the expense of the truck rental. Frank had not shown up during the move, she told me. I wanted to confide in her, to lighten the load of my appointment with Meara, but I sensed I had better not.

Carolina was wearing some garish make-up she had smeared on her face at transition house. Simone, a feminist and naturalist, looked at the make-up with disgust and asked Carolina to take it off.

Carolina refused. "No! Then people will know who I am!" She climbed up on my lap and added, "I'm tired, Mommy. But when I sleep, I don't have you. I don't have a mommy at all."

When we got back to transition house, I told Carolina about the child abuse interview, hoping to prepare her. To ensure her attention, I held her shoulders. I said, "You don't have to talk about this with anyone but Roma."

Carolina twisted away. "Well, I'm not. You tell her. It's not my fault. I told you everything. You can tell her. I'm not going to talk. I don't have any more to say. I told you already. You're supposed to take care of me, you know."

"This appointment with Roma is so that I can."

"Mom, it's your fault. You took all my words for saying stuff. I don't have any left. I don't have to talk. It's my decision."

Flopping down on the bed, she hiked up her dress and spread her legs. She pulled two drinking straws up to her genitals. "I want to see Daddy. See my big vagina, Mommy? The big boys can't look at me and touch me if I say no, can they, Mom? My vagina is big as a house."

Amy ate. Blessedly, after nearly three days, Amy ate. She accepted a bottle.

12

WHILE WE WERE EATING a late breakfast a few days later, a worker named Sue came in to sit with us, saying she wanted to talk. Great, I thought, biting into some toast.

"There's not much help available," Sue said, "and you need to start accepting that, Ellen."

I couldn't believe what I was hearing. "Accept that because of a flawed system my kids go to their dad and he hurts them again?"

"Getting yourself in such a dander doesn't help anyone," she said.

I flung my toast down. "Why does everyone say I should calm down?" I said, ignoring the fact that moments before I *had* been calm. "When I do calm down you think I'm unnatural. If I'm emotional, I'm hysterical. If I'm cogent, you think I'm intellectualizing. If I'm angry you think I'm overreacting. If I'm not angry you say that in my shoes you'd be damned pissed off."

"That's not true, Ellen, and you know it."

"It's not true?" I'd been gesticulating and now I put my hands palm down on the tabletop.

Sue was silent.

Measuredly, I said, "I've read the notes the staff has been writing."

Her face blanched. "You read our notes? On whose authority?"

"Marie's."

There was a pause. "You've been here eight days," she said. Then, awkwardly, "We want to offer you a move to Lowther House."

"What's that?"

"A second-stage transition house run by the YWCA. You'll have your own apartment, and the stay can be as long as six months." She scratched her head. "Because it sounds to the staff here that you're serious about not going back to your husband. Do you have other plans?"

I shook my head.

"Think it over. They have a spot for you. Think about it and let us know." She left abruptly.

I wondered what I should do. The thought of disappearing south over the border—to my mother's, say—was tantalizing. And while Amy was probably oblivious, Carolina had seen too much here, too many brutalized women and traumatized kids. Maybe in Lowther House things would settle back to normal, whatever that was. Maybe.

I decided I'd try it.

The next day, leaving the kids with the homemaker, I attended a meeting of a group for mothers of sexually abused children. It was my first contact with women in a similar situation; nine of us and two therapists sat around a boardroom table trying to understand how we had come to be here, and why. I was shy and quiet, but I listened intently to what the therapists had to say:

Sexual abuse is often intergenerational. Survivors of it can grow to love men who mirror the abuser.

Abuse is a euphemism for the word rape.

Men rape children because children are powerless.

If a father has abused his children, the community assumes the mother is somehow responsible: she's frigid, castrating, passive, domineering or absent. Mothers, who actually know of the abuse only in rare instances, are said to "collude" in it.

"I wasn't there," a mom named Peggy wailed. "How could I

collude when I wasn't even there?" Her seven-year-old son had been hurt by her brother-in-law.

As I listened, identifying, I felt a deep repulsion. I didn't think all men raped kids, not by a long shot, but the ones who did made my skin crawl. I had a fantasy, freak and fast, of castration, of chopping off men's penises, one after another, a long, satisfying burst of retributive justice. Frank was first in line. Then I moved to territory that usually overcame me only late at night, making the pictures of what Frank had done.

"The point is," a therapist said, "what we've been trying to tell you, is that you're *not* responsible." She slapped the table to emphasize her point. "It's a set-up. These guys work to alienate moms from their children. There are all sorts of behaviour problems, and the men capitalize on that, blaming the wife. And sooner or later, the relationship between the mom and kids has gone to pot. Abusers count on that."

That sounded like Frank, too. I could see all too well that in another five or ten years with him around, I would have become deeply estranged from the girls. I whispered, "I won't ever, ever stop feeling guilty."

"None of us will," Peggy said, leaning forward.

"Maybe," the other therapist acknowledged, "but remember, you didn't make your husbands or partners do this. You really didn't. No one has that much control over someone else."

Reasonable, but I still had my feelings to deal with, and they were deep, wild and raw. It wasn't as easy as what made sense. I'd failed my children—that was the crux of the matter.

But it was heartening, later in the session, to hear that early intervention—stopping the abuse and getting therapy—could put children's lives back together.

Carolina ran sobbing into our room, where I was packing for the move to Lowther House. "Men!" she yelled. "Quick, Mommy, help!"

In the hallway were plumbers heading to fix some leaky pipes. I'd been told they were coming; it never occurred to me to let Carolina know.

From the outside, Lowther House looked haunted. Inside, it was just an ordinary house divided into six one- or two-bedroom apartments. Residents had to share the phone in the second-floor hallway and the TV in the basement common room, but otherwise we lived independently. The first-floor office was staffed weekdays by two hospitable, warm women named Laura and Ethel who made me feel instantly at home. The attic suite Ethel showed us to was small, terribly hot and fully furnished. After an orientation chat, she left us to get settled in.

Right away, Carolina had me tack up another list of rules:

No men.

Bedtime at eight.

No hitting Amy.

Marie called from transition house to say that I'd really shaken the place up. Fractiousness in the ranks, she called it, and said they were working on sexual abuse protocol. I wondered whether knowing we'd been guinea pigs was supposed to cheer me up.

After a few days, Carolina said, "I want to call Daddy and get Blankie."

"Yeah?" I said cautiously, by now my normal approach to Carolina's disturbing utterances. It was important, I thought, to compile as many of them as possible, in case they might help keep the girls safe, but they still hurt deeply; I dreaded them.

"No, you call him. If I call him he'll come here and get me." Her delivery was flat, as if she were discussing something mundane, not something obscenely wrong.

I closed my eyes. "No, he won't, Carolina. He's not allowed here."

"Do you have a list?"

I was sitting at our kitchen table, sweating in the July heat. "A shopping list?" I pushed a piece of paper towards her.

She drew squiggles. "There. That says buy me a new blanket, Mommy."

Later that day, we did.

Meara and I sat with Sally March in the district office of the Ministry of Human Resources. It was a little more than two weeks since I had reported the abuse. Carolina was off in another room being interviewed by Roma Flagge, from the Ministry's child abuse team, and a plainclothes policeman, a Constable Mills. On pins and needles, I asked, "Has Roma got the skills to figure out whether or not this really happened?"

Meara frowned, and Sally didn't reply.

"Because I want it not to be true, Sally. I keep imagining what it must have been like." I covered my face, overwhelmed.

Meara said, "Just hang on, Ellen. However it goes in there, it'll be over soon."

"Carolina called Frank from a play phone this morning. You know what she said? 'Daddy, you're not allowed to hurt me any more. It's a rule from women.' Then she ran in to breakfast saying she'd talked to her father and he said he wouldn't come and get her."

Sally nodded. "She's establishing boundaries: 'Here is the line, Daddy, that you can't step over.' She's helping *you* establish boundaries."

"She said she likes the rules women make." I hesitated. "But you know what the weirdest thing is? I miss Frank. I do. I'm sorry, but it's the truth. I've known him for a long time."

After that, we just waited. When Carolina came out, I was so happy to see her I grabbed her up and twirled her.

Roma Flagge called the next day while Amy was asleep and Carolina was playing with neighbours' children. I gave Roma my full attention; a lot was riding on what she said.

Roma said that Carolina was very frightened of doctors and

men. "Where would she get those fears, Ellen?" she asked, her voice tainted with suspicion.

I was surprised. "Well, transition house and Lowther House. I mean, there's a definite sense of men being the enemy. Also, you know, well ... her dad's a man."

"Do you hate men?"

Wearily, I said, as I had to Sally March, "No, I don't hate men." I tangled the phone cord. "Look, Carolina was never scared of men before now. She was nervous about going to her father's, but otherwise, no, absolutely not."

Roma made an assessing noise in her throat. "And the fear of doctors?"

"Dr. Cole scared her. I know Dr. Cole thought Carolina was comfortable, but she wasn't, she was terrified."

"She's very clear that she loves her father. She denied sexual abuse, said her father only 'hit' her and 'kicked' her."

I was quiet.

"But I used anatomically correct dolls with her, and she liked that they had all their parts. She took the little girl doll and repeatedly played at putting things in its vagina and saying 'Pain, pain, pain.'"

I swallowed. I wasn't expecting to hear something so graphic.

"Which convinced me someone has certainly hurt Carolina vaginally. That was evident. I gather that's in concurrence with the physician's findings?"

"Yes," I said.

"You told Sally March that there were no other men in her life besides her father?"

"Well, no, not in any but a casual way. The staff at the daycare were all female. Her uncles sometimes visit. But otherwise, no."

"Were you seeing anyone, Ellen? Dating? I gather you and Carolina's father were separated?"

"I was, yes. But he was never alone with the kids. We weren't that serious."

"You're trained, I gather, in psychology?"

Puzzled, I told her I was.

"Well, I'm wondering, then, if you used your training?"

"I don't get what you mean," I said carefully.

"If you coached Carolina?"

"Coached her?" I bit my lip, hard.

There was a pause, an abrupt change of subject. "Why did you bring your lawyer to Carolina's interview?"

"Meara? She offered to come."

"It's unusual," Roma said.

I waited.

"Meara is a surprising choice of attorney, wouldn't you say?"

"You're confusing me," I said. "What are you asking?" But then I got it, though Roma had moved on. Meara was a lesbian—that's what made her "surprising."

"Carolina's a darling child. Very precocious, very bright. I enjoyed seeing her. There's a book I want you to get called *Where Did I Come From?* that explains human reproduction. I'd like you to go over it with Carolina."

I agreed, but I was distracted. I wanted her to go back to Meara, to say what she seemed to think, that if Meara was a lesbian, I probably was too—which in her eyes would explain a lot.

"And generally, you know, normalize your situation."

I thought of being stuck in a shelter, how normal that was.

"Don't question Carolina. Don't talk about sexual abuse in front of her. Answer her questions as honestly as you can, but minimize abuse. She needs to be a normal little girl."

"Of course," I said woodenly.

"Are you still seeing your boyfriend?"

"No," I said. I hadn't called anyone, not Barry, not Teresa or Jean or my mother or my brother.

Roma cut the conversation off abruptly. "Nice talking with you, Ellen. My interview with Carolina was a pleasure."

"Right," I said.

"I'll be talking to you again."

It sounded like a threat.

I was frustrated when I hung up, full of warring emotions. There was lots of subtext in my conversation with Roma, as there had been with Sally, the doctor and the transition house workers. After these talks, each rife with innuendo and insinuation, I spent hours mulling. I didn't want to be seen as a "client," someone from whom information was routinely withheld; I wanted to be treated as a fully participating partner in piecing together what had happened to my children. But past that, I felt the weight of accusation never fully voiced, unanswerable because unspoken. I felt broadsided and didn't know how to protect myself.

Some of the insinuations I recognized as bigotry, but some hit home, bruising me in the places where I was insecure and needy. The one that told me I was somehow at fault was one I readily assumed. Was I? I asked myself again and again.

That night I read Carolina a Care Bears story. She was quiet and ready for sleep; I pushed tendrils of damp hair away from her forehead.

"Mommy?"

"Mmm?"

"I didn't tell Roma about Daddy. I made a fib."

I sighed. What she called her fib was likely to have severe consequences, but I said, "That's okay, sugarbear. You told me you weren't going to. You were brave anyway."

"Do I have to worry about Roma getting hurt?"

Roma getting hurt? I was constantly amazed at how Carolina's mind worked. Poor darling, I thought. Poor *baby*. "No one's going to hurt Roma, I promise," I said softly.

"'Cause maybe Dad will."

"No, Carolina, he won't," I promised, ignoring the ache in my chest.

"He could."

"Go to sleep, sweetie pie. Close your eyes." I started humming a lullaby.

"He could come here with a gun."

A gun. Jesus. Why this constant fear of guns? Had Frank

threatened her with a gun? "Everyone's safe, Carolina. Everyone's safe." I hummed and stroked her temples. A *gun*, I thought over and over as she drifted to sleep.

Later that night I read in a local women's newspaper about a weekend at a nearby lake being offered for bisexual women and their children. It piqued my interest. I was desperate to get away, and if I didn't exactly consider myself bisexual, it didn't seem to matter, not for a weekend of camping. All it would cost was gas and food, which I could manage. I felt brave and foolhardy calling the contact number.

Now that we were somewhat settled in at Lowther House, I arranged to drop back to Susan's to pick up the boxes I'd housed in her storage locker. I wouldn't be able to take everything in one trip, but at least I could find books and music and basic toys. Since I'd lost my emergency homemaker—I'd apparently moved out of "crisis"—wherever I went, Carolina and Amy went, tugging along their needs.

Susan's back was still giving her trouble, she said. She sank into her recliner, grumpy and pained. Though she didn't offer tea, I sat, too, but the atmosphere was strained. Amy and Carolina were into everything, grabbing at the buttons on Susan's stereo and using her cassettes as cymbals. I tucked Amy under my arm and hollered at Carolina to stop fingering Susan's stone dolls, but then I saw Susan's sour expression. "We'd better get going," I said. "I just have to move my car around front."

"I can't get up to buzz you in again," Susan groused.

"That's okay. Susan, I truly appreciate what you've done for us. I'm very thankful."

The air was full of tension. I asked Susan to watch the girls while I went down to unlock the storage room and move the car, but she refused and so I borrowed her keys. The girls and I rode down the elevator, back up to drop off the keys, and down again. I moved the car around to the entrance, left Amy in her car seat, went back in and shouldered boxes into the hallway without sorting them.

Slowly, I kicked and knocked and carried boxes towards the double doors.

I had Carolina hold the door for me. I could hear Amy crying and someone yelling. A man shouted that my car was in the way.

I hucked boxes fast, knowing I couldn't get back in if the door shut behind me.

Suddenly, three or four of Susan's neighbours were screaming obscenities at each other.

"Stay here, Carolina," I yelled and ran out. I moved my car, pulling it up closer to the entrance. Though I was no longer blocking the driveway, the commotion continued. I jammed boxes into the car and shoved Carolina in on top of them. Susan appeared on her balcony, yelling too and shaking her fist at her neighbours.

Whatever this was, it had gone way past just me blocking traffic. Everyone had forgotten me, even Susan, so, worried about violence, I left, puttering out as fast as my small Volkswagen could carry us. I was shaky, perplexed and disoriented for the rest of the afternoon.

Susan called that evening. I ran down to the phone, thinking we'd commiserate, but her voice was pitched tight. "I don't know for what crazy reason you set that up, but you set it up."

It was so unexpected I gasped.

"You set me up. I had to go back and apologize to those people. Those people were waiting for you to move your car."

I tried to explain I *had* moved it as soon as I'd realized.

"You turn dependent when it suits you and oh-so-capable when it doesn't," Susan accused. "I don't appreciate being set up. I don't appreciate your behaviour as a guest in my house. How you let your kids run amuck through all my stuff."

She hung up. I stared at the phone that had gone dead in my hand.

I was aghast. I dialled Brigit, thinking I'd spill this curious wreck of a story when she answered. The line was busy for some time, but at last it rang free.

"Oh," Brigit said when she heard it was me. Her voice was flattened by caution. "Ellen."

"I just had the strangest call from Susan," I said, ignoring her tone. "You won't believe this, Brigit." Then I stopped; it occurred to me that the busy signal was perhaps because she and Susan had been talking. "Did you talk to her?"

"No," Brigit said carefully. "What happened?"

"Okay, well. I went over there to get some of my stuff, right? And her neighbours ... this is hard to explain. I'd blocked the parking lot entrance, only I didn't know it, and then these people started screaming, Brigit, I mean *screaming*, death threats even, but I don't know how it got so out of hand, and—"

Brigit cut me off. "Susan got things straightened out," she said protectively.

I stuttered, "You just said you didn't talk to her!"

Brigit sighed. "She didn't think she could, but she did. She apologized to everyone."

My mouth fell open, but I didn't say anything.

"I have to go," Brigit said. "You caught me at a bad time. I'm busy."

"I—"

"Good-bye," she said.

"Brigit!" I said, but she'd hung up.

I tried to write out the pain of these events in my journal, but it hit me at an inchoate level. I was struggling anyway, with the kids' abuse, in a place where language seemed to be my enemy, where my thoughts and feelings were so tangled and complex that I couldn't unravel them, couldn't write a cogent sentence past a scant, factual recounting. What could I possibly say about Susan and Brigit? All I could do was take wild, metaphoric leaps full of images of blood, because that's what the turning away of my friends felt like. Like whatever grip on reality I'd had during this crisis was now wrenched away, like Susan and Brigit had slit me open and left me to die, like I was walking and talking and parenting my children, but I was dead.

How could this be happening? It had to be my fault.

13

I HELD THE women's weekend at Cultus Lake against myself as a sort of talisman. If I'd been a drinker, I suppose I would have gone on a binge, but failing that, I could only think of escape, of leaving the city, of forgetting, for a couple of days, my lonely situation.

On the two-hour drive east—I caught a lift with one of the organizers—I told myself I was a damned fool, and when we arrived at a crude lodge deep in the woods and I was assigned two rudimentary bunks in a room without electricity, I roundly cursed myself. Carolina and Amy were timid, but not as timid as I was among these confident strangers. I wished I hadn't come; I wished I were invisible.

The first evening, outside around a campfire, I hardly noticed that the night was warm and the sky freckled with stars. Instead, I sat on a stump as far from the group as I could politely get and attended my children. Amy's nose was stuffy and she was crying a lot. When I could logically excuse myself to put the girls to bed, I did so, creeping into the dark, empty lodge with a flashlight, fussing over the kids.

The next morning, after a breakfast of pancakes I hardly noticed because Amy had developed full cold symptoms and diarrhea during the night and now needed constant changing and soothing, the group headed to a stony, half-moon beach on the lake. I sat apart from the others again, watching while women took off their tops. I no longer knew where to look. I couldn't exactly stare at their breasts, but I couldn't exactly not stare, either, and I shot out covert glances under the cover of fetching Carolina, who repeatedly wandered towards the water.

Back at the lodge, I ran out of both diapers and rash cream, and Amy's bowels kept emptying. There was desultory talk about making a diaper run for me, but I knew that wasn't a solution. Amy needed baths and central heating. Finally a woman named Denise, who was sitting uncomfortably close to me, suggested we drive back to her house in the Fraser Valley.

When she grinned at me in the car, explaining she had small kids herself, I felt rescued. Denise had a disordered mop of long, nearly white hair, a large, lopsided smile, and an intense stare that she fastened on me at regular intervals. She wore a blue satin cowboy shirt and jeans, and around her waist, a studded black belt. I watched her fingers curl over the steering wheel; her short nails were painted bright red. She lived in Port Coquitlam, where she ran a group home. We latched onto work as a topic of easy discussion, and before I knew it we were picking up supplies at a corner grocery, then pulling into Denise's driveway.

"I'll take you into the city tomorrow," she promised with a big crooked smile. Her teeth were exceptionally white. She turned off the ignition and we sat assessing each other until one of her workers rapped on the car window.

Our evening was filled to the brim with child care; besides her son, nine, and daughter, seven, Denise cared for three developmentally disabled kids. We made it through the chaos of dinner, dishes and bedtimes, putting Carolina down with Denise's daughter and Amy in a playpen, the other children in their various bedrooms.

Denise opened a bottle of wine; I accepted a glass while she built a fire.

For a while we were uncomfortable, but gradually our talk deepened and grew more intimate. Haltingly, I told her about Carolina and Amy's abuse; she countered with stories of the abuse she'd suffered at the hands of her father. She told me she'd been married but had had an affair with a woman and then divorced. I admitted I had no idea if I was bisexual. She laughed and said she didn't know that about herself, either, but that she thought she was probably a lesbian.

I drew in my breath.

"I didn't rescue you, you know," she said, amused. "It was a pickup."

I stuttered something about how I couldn't... I didn't... I wasn't... but she pulled me into her arms and kissed me so softly it stole my breath.

Then, as I protested, she took my hand and led me into her bedroom, locking the door.

"I can't ... *sleep* with you," I said.

"No," she nodded, "just lie beside me."

I got stiffly into bed, aware of little besides Denise's smoky, wine-soaked breath, her face inches from mine, her hands stroking my arms.

"I don't know what to do," I whispered.

"Shh," Denise said and laid a finger against my lips. "I'll show you everything."

"But I... "

"Kiss me," she said, her voice full of desire.

Her breasts were against my breasts, so soft. "I thought we were just... I don't think I'm a... I mean, I'm not a... "

"I know," she said.

She kissed me and I fell into it, returning it, exploring her warm, wet mouth. Her hand touched my right breast, a hint of a caress, and I felt a shock of deep pleasure.

"I don't know how—" I said, but she silenced me, unbuttoning my shirt.

"Lie back," she said, "let me teach you."

In my journal, I recorded ambivalence about my night with Denise. On the one hand, I was gratified to have finally stepped over a line I'd been longing all my life to cross, but on the other I was shaken by Denise's intensity and made uncomfortable by how deeply affirming and restorative I'd found it. I didn't think I deserved the pleasure it had aroused in me and I felt guilty because Denise and I were virtual strangers and because it could jeopardize my daughters' safety if anyone found out. But at certain moments I just felt stubbornly good; I'd catch myself humming or singing, floating through the kitchen with a stupid grin glued to my face.

"Do you want to go back to daycare?" I asked Carolina one morning.

"Yeah," she said, "but tell Daddy he's not allowed to pick me up, okay?"

"Yes, of course," I said, "that would be the rule. I'll talk to your teachers about it."

"Will the police put a gun at Daddy's head?" Carolina asked.

It was futile to try and keep anything from her. Or maybe Roma had told her the police would be involved. "Oh, no, honey, they won't hurt him. They'll only tell Daddy the rules."

"Yeah, Daddy doesn't know the rules. Will they put on handcuffs?"

"They'll only talk to him about the rule that daddies can't hurt their daughters."

"With their penis. It's a rule."

"Yes, that's a big rule, all right. Daddies aren't allowed to touch their daughters with their penises."

"Daddy won't hurt Roma?"

"No, uh-uh," I reiterated. "Daddy won't hurt Roma."

"He might."

"Nope," I said firmly. "I promise."

"Can I play with Sammy?"

I hadn't called Barry. "Not yet, Carolina."

"Is she bad, so I can't play with her?"

"No, Carolina. Sammy's not bad at all."

"Then why?"

"Oh, honey," I said. This was too much for breakfast conversation. I looked over at Amy drinking her bottle. "It's not your fault or Sammy's. It's just the way things are for now. I'm sorry. It's just how things have got to be."

"I want to see Sammy. Can I have more French toast, Mommy?"

At the end of the week I called Frank. I was at one of the low points I often hit, thinking that Carolina was making it up, that all that was troubling her was my mothering, and I missed him. My mothers' group called this "denial," but I still wanted ... something. His reassurance? To know I was wrong? To know we could go back to the way things had been?

He said he'd been looking for me. He'd been to Carolina's daycare, to Simone's, to Brigit's, to the apartment I'd leased. "Do you need money?" he asked. "Can I get you anything?"

I told him I'd gone away "to think." His voice was so normal, so ordinary, that imagining him as an offender was impossible. But the contact unnerved me. This wasn't a game. I was hiding from him. That was the truth of things. I was running from him on behalf of my two little girls.

"I'm sorry," I said quietly and hung up.

Downstairs, Marnie's five-year-old daughter, Suzanne, returned from a visiting weekend with her father and step-brother ripped from stem to stern. Though she needed seven stitches to close her vagina, there was no change to her visitation: come Friday, Suzanne was to go back. According to her father, Suzanne had fallen on a toy. During her child abuse interview she crawled under a table and screamed.

I called Barry.

"Ellen!" he said. "Where are you? Frank's been out of his mind."

"You've been talking to Frank?" I asked cautiously. I had called to see if it was safe for Carolina to see Sammy.

"Frank says you just love heavy trips."

Do I? I wondered. Do I? "Why were you talking to Frank? You barely know him."

"Franks says you've gone off to become a lesbian."

"What?" I felt a stab of guilt. Did he know about Denise somehow?

"He says your friend Simone is a lesbian."

"So?" I said.

"So you're going to get lost in a forest, Ellen."

I was getting mad. "Barry, that's ridiculous."

"What did Frank ever do to you?"

"Good-bye, Barry."

"Call me when you come to your senses."

"Good-bye," I said, with emphasis.

Kevin Mills, the detective assigned to our case, finally called to set up an appointment. I was very nervous, but I turned over the pages of Carolina's initial disclosures to him.

"Have you arranged a second interview with Roma?" he asked.

"We're seeing her tomorrow," I confirmed.

"Yes," he said, "she mentioned that."

Anger flashed through me, then despair. Did they think I was totally untrustworthy, I wondered, or just stupid?

The kids and I dropped by Simone's that afternoon. Carolina complained of a sore crotch, and I found her wiping herself in the bathroom, "even though I didn't pee, Mom."

"Mention it to Roma tomorrow, okay, sugar?"

"My dad didn't hurt me," she said angrily.

I felt my patience slipping away. Simone had told me that when Frank came looking for us she'd invited him in for tea. I asked her if she'd told him why we'd disappeared, and she admitted she had. I watched Carolina pull up her pants. I said, "Look, Carolina, if Daddy didn't hurt you, we'd better apologize to him. Because what we're saying is really mean if it's not true."

"He didn't."

"Okay. Fine," I said.

"He did so. He did hurt me with his penis. He did not."

Unable to stop myself, I said, "Which is it? What about your bum?"

"How do you know about my bum?"

"You told me," I reminded her.

"I don't care. He didn't hurt me. Leave me alone."

I clenched my teeth and thought, if I'm wrong, I don't know how to make it up. I could never make it up to anyone.

After Carolina's second interview with Roma Flagge, I asked, "Anything?"

"Nothing," Roma said, shaking her head. "I should have videotaped that first session, because Carolina was very convincing."

I stared at her.

"Carolina was *very* convincing," she repeated. She raised her palms, shrugged and smiled, as if to say it didn't really matter, then reached out to pat Carolina's head.

I had a flash desire to shake Roma. She said she wanted to talk to me some more, and we scheduled a meeting over tea.

The day I put Carolina back in daycare, I found out from one of the daycare workers that I had missed Frank by minutes. It scared me cold. But the staff, believing Frank to be "the type," assured me that they wouldn't release Carolina to him. Frank could kidnap her, but I didn't think he'd try it. Shakily, I bet he wouldn't.

That evening I read a list of child victims' feelings I'd gotten at my mothers' group to a rapt Carolina. I wanted her to know her thoughts and fears were normal. The pamphlet spoke of children continuing to tell adults until they found an adult who would help them.

"Yeah," said Carolina. "You and Roma."

"That's right," I told her encouragingly.

"Only I didn't tell Roma."

"I know."

Carolina looked at me sharply. "You didn't get mad when I told you, did you?"

"No, sweetheart, not mad at all."

"I better keep talking about it or Daddy will hurt me again."

"I think it helps to keep talking about it," I agreed. I'd been trying to line up some therapy for myself and the girls but was having no luck. I was wavering in and out of a fear-laden depression: *could* I keep the girls safe? And could I cope regardless? I'd lost Frank, and then Susan and Barry and Brigit; could I cope? I gave silent thanks for Denise. "But you're safe, Carolina. I'm not going to let Daddy hurt you again whether or not you talk about it."

It was my one absolute. Regardless of what happened in the legal arena—and supposedly only 10 per cent of offenders were charged, and a scant 10 per cent of those convicted—I was not going to let Frank hurt his children again.

A wave of resentment washed over me. I resented losing my home and my friends. I resented my fear and the girls' trauma, the extra patience parenting them required. I resented having my life an open book, with police and social workers turning the pages. I resented that I was dependent on social services. I resented my lack of access to our records. I resented that even though I hadn't done anything wrong, I was in the government's spotlight and Frank was not. I resented that Frank wasn't behind bars.

Carolina had trouble settling. She asked if I'd lie down with her. She grabbed my hand and pushed it, hard, towards her crotch. I resisted. She pushed harder and said, "*Put* your hand."

I said, "No, I won't."

Carolina's tone became whiny and desperate. "Put it!"

"No, I won't," I said firmly.

"You have to. I like it!"

"No, absolutely not. It's abuse."

"Why?" Carolina wailed.

"It's against the rules," I said firmly.

"It's okay if kids *like* it."

"No, it's not, Carolina. It's okay for kids to like being touched there but it's not okay for adults to touch them. If an adult does, the adult is bad."

Carolina turned away from me. In a haunted voice she intoned, "My daddy's bad."

Meara called me with the contents of Dr. Cole's report. It said that Carolina's vaginal and anal walls "gaped"; a smear for the presence of sperm was "inconclusive."

Meara had also spoken to Roma Flagge. In her interviews with Roma, Carolina had drawn pictures. Her artwork was anatomically correct except for her figures' mouths, which were absent or wavy. Roma told Meara that children involved in fellatio often had difficulty drawing mouths. Carolina masturbated when she saw the anatomical dolls. She identified the adult male doll as "Daddy" and grabbed his penis. When she played with the little girl doll, she told Roma it was pregnant. She took a play spoon, told Roma it contained "sperm" and had the little girl doll drink it. When Roma asked who got the little girl doll pregnant, Carolina said it was her daddy. Then Carolina took a pair of scissors from Roma's desk and inserted them into the little girl doll's vagina. Over and over she repeated, shoving them deeper and harder and asking for Roma's help, "It has to hurt! It has to hurt!"

My little girl, no taller than a kitchen counter.

Roma's conclusions were that Carolina had been sexually assaulted. She could not say by whom. To err on the side of caution, she recommended that Frank be refused custody and unsupervised visits. Should Frank be granted access, she said, the ministry would launch an emergency investigation into his fitness as a parent. Roma believed that the offender was probably Frank but told Meara that, in the absence of a statement from Carolina confirming it, she could not be positive.

"I've checked into the possibility of Carolina testifying against Frank," Meara said. "Remember I said I would?"

"Yes?" I asked guardedly, still reluctant.

"A child has to convince a judge that she's competent. It's unlikely a judge would decide that about Carolina because of her age. So it's as I told you."

"Frank gets away with it?"

"Unless we find a witness, Carolina's testimony, even allowed and corroborated, wouldn't be enough for a conviction." Meara fell silent. "Also, Roma had a talk with Sally March and they've decided you've been overreacting, Ellen."

"Overreacting?" I said and gave a barking laugh. I thought of Carolina in Roma's office offering sperm to a doll, then of Frank.

"She wants you to get therapy. She says you're not child-focussed."

"What's *that* mean?"

Meara laughed. "I haven't got the slightest clue."

When I met with Roma the next day, she went over the same ground Meara had covered, adding that Carolina was deeply unhappy. Carolina displayed "inappropriately adult behaviour," Roma said, age-unlikely fears of doctors, police and men.

"She *is* the oldest child," I said defensively. "Oldest kids are always precocious."

Roma bit into the muffin she'd ordered. "Was Frank sexually abused as a child?" she asked.

I told her that he'd been raised Catholic, in a home with corporal punishment. I mentioned the incident with the nuns—he had been four, I said. Otherwise, I didn't know.

"I'd be willing to swear an affidavit declaring that Carolina was vaginally abused," Roma said, licking butter from her fingers.

I nodded.

"Oh, and the ministry is prepared to absorb the cost of six therapy sessions."

"For Carolina? That's wonderful."

"No," she said, "for you."

"For me?" I lifted my eyebrows.

Roma stared hard. "We think you need therapy."

"I *know* I need therapy," I agreed. "And a lot more than six sessions, too. But so does Carolina."

"I've spoken to a woman named Gloria Keefer who's agreed to see you."

"Will the ministry cover the cost of my mothers' group? Or therapy for Carolina if I can find someone?"

"We may be able to get Carolina on a contract with a child-care worker at a neighbourhood house," Roma said.

"Roma, that's like sending a cancer patient to a massage therapist."

Roma shrugged. "As for the mothers' group, no, we won't cover the cost. We wouldn't have sent you there. It's a bit out of line with reality."

Maybe *your* reality, I thought bitterly. But I kept my mouth shut.

I liked Gloria Keefer. She was older and motherly and empathic. In the first session, held on a houseboat, I filled her in on our situation. But during the second session, I fell into the wash of my own memories, then jerked shakily back to tell her about Lowther House, how Carolina had been yelled at by another mother for running around nude, how she'd played doctor with a little girl while I was in the basement doing laundry and how the mom who had found them shunned us now.

Kids could act out their abuse on other children, Gloria told me. I should be particularly watchful when Carolina was around younger children. It was a new and disturbing worry that ran smack up against my defences. I wasn't going to believe Carolina was capable of hurting anyone, I just wasn't.

I changed the subject, telling Gloria about how one of the moms at Lowther House had had her kids dragged away screaming for visiting weekends with the father that had battered her and kidnapped them. "By social workers," I added pointedly. "Ordered to do it by the court."

The child-care worker assigned to Carolina was a teen-ager named Joyce, who came to Lowther House to meet Carolina just before taking off on a month's vacation. I sat with Amy while she and Carolina talked in the bedroom. After a few minutes, Carolina burst from the room and flung herself from the apartment.

I started a family history with Joyce. Within minutes, though, Carolina stomped back in and slammed into her room. A mother named Martha came up the stairs behind her, carrying her crying son Adam. "Bite marks," she said, holding up his arm. There were teeth marks there, all right.

I marched Carolina out and made her apologize. Her voice was squeaky with humiliation.

Meara called to tell me that the police had interrogated Frank. Finally, after six weeks. But I heard nothing that day about how the interview had gone.

At bedtime I mentioned to Carolina that the police had told her dad the rules.

"I want a bottle, Mommy," she said. "Can I have Amy's bottle?"

I cuddled her.

Nervously, she asked, "Mommy, are the policemen going to talk to me?"

"No," I assured her.

"To you?"

"Just to Daddy. Are you scared, Carolina, that they'll hurt him?"

"No."

"Scared they'll hurt you?"

"Yes. And you too, Mommy. 'Cause you and him did the same thing."

"You mean Daddy and I did the same thing that Daddy did to you?" Sex? She'd just read *Where Did I Come From?*

"Right. If I was big I'd just fight them off, 'cept for Daddy."

"If you were big," I echoed, not understanding her.

"Right."

"You'd fight them off. But not Daddy. Who would you fight off, sweetie?"

"Men, 'cause I'll get hurt."

"No one will hurt you, love, I promise."

"'Cause then I'd be big. It doesn't hurt if you're big. Only 'cause I'm little it stuck in me."

"You're okay now, Carolina," I said softly.

Constable Mills called the next morning.

I asked him if Frank was okay. First, like an idiot, I asked that.

"He was surprised," Mills replied.

"What did he say?"

"I'm not at liberty to divulge that. But I wanted you to know we've talked to him. The investigation's continuing, and you're involved."

I felt a sharp stab of fear, but when he asked me to, I agreed to keep him up to date on Carolina's disclosures.

I called Sally March. She wouldn't, couldn't, tell me much about what had happened either. I'd expected to hear. I'd been waiting to hear. Sally let slip that Frank had offered both to take a polygraph and to be interviewed by a worker from the Ministry of Human Resources. She said Constable Mills had told her that Frank was "a hard guy to read" and that he had said "several suspicious things." Mills had the impression something sexual had happened between Frank and Carolina. Beyond that I was stonewalled.

"Did I mention that Dr. Cole's report says Carolina has a stretched hymen?" Sally added. She sounded sympathetic, and I wondered if she was becoming an ally.

I waited.

"Sexual abuse is in her opinion evident."

"Yes," I said dryly, "it's evident to me, too."

14

NOT KNOWING IF it was the right thing to do, I decided to leave Lowther House. Displaced and fearful, the residents fought among themselves. And twice a week or so, in response to a woman seeing or hearing something suspicious, an alarm went up. Officers descended. We were roused from our beds so that room searches could be held. We stood in the lobby in robes and slippers, babies and kids in our arms, awaiting the all clear.

I needed something more normal, and the kids did too. Though I was always scared, I needed to start depending more on myself and less on the government; I had to bet on Frank continuing to leave us be.

I signed a lease on a new apartment for September first.

Meara called to say that Frank had retained a lawyer rather than submitting to a polygraph. He had also refused to be interviewed by Ministry officials.

Carolina asked me to read *Where Did I Come From?* again. In the book, sex was described as a pleasurable activity. Reasons were given why adults don't make love all the time. One of them was that sex was like being tickled—a little went a long way.

Carolina said, "The second one is because something happens then that hurts you?"

"Pumpkin," I said, tired of having to talk about it, "it only hurts if it's bad touching, like between a grownup and a child."

"I *like* making love with Daddy," she said. "It feels good. But you still should've been there."

"Yeah, I know," I said. "I wouldn't have let him. But I didn't know."

"You knew when I was telling you on the phone, though, and crying."

As I had before, I searched my memory futilely for such an occasion. "No," I said, "I really didn't know. I'll keep you safe, though, now that I do know."

"We just sucked each other and kissed."

"Oh," I said, "oh."

"Sucking penises tastes yucky, Mommy, and Daddy never wiped himself after peeing and I wouldn't suck him unless he did and he never did." She looked up at my troubled face. "We never sucked each other."

I felt dizzy.

"Mom, if two little girls put their lips together, could they make a baby?"

"Uh-uh."

"Two fourteen-year-old girls?"

"Nope."

"Their private part lips?"

Was she talking about having been found playing doctor? "No."

"A grownup man and a little girl?"

"No."

"A grownup woman and a little girl?"

"No."

Then she said, "Two grownup women?"

"No," I said, hoping against hope because of Denise that she was just requesting information.

After I got Carolina off to sleep, I sat in the living room and thought about Denise and what she meant to me. We'd been together three or four more times, but because she lived outside of the city, only our phone contact was regular. She was a huge support to me, and I knew I counted on her. I knew I needed her. But was I in love? Denise said she was, but I didn't know about myself. She aroused intense feelings in me, certainly, but my feelings weren't sortable. All I could do was go along with her, seeing where time took us, and for the most part this seemed to be acceptable to Denise.

I'd told Meara about her, since I knew Frank had used lesbianism to explain our distance to Barry. Meara wanted to find out if Frank had also told the police; if he had, homophobia might raise its head and influence the disposition of our case. That a child abuser could go free because a woman slept with other women made me profoundly sad and angry, but Meara said it would be a long time before homosexuality went unremarked. She advised me to keep my affair with Denise hidden.

I hadn't talked to my mother about what was going on, unable to take the chance of another rejection. But after Frank was questioned by the police, I felt I had to call her in case he did.

I began by telling her haltingly about my own abuse, gritting my teeth, minimalizing my many memories. I really expected her to say I was crazy.

But after a long sad stretch of quiet, she sighed, "Oh, Ellen, I knew you were a deeply unhappy little girl," she said. "But I ... I just thought you wanted to be left alone."

She said it was like I'd handed her a key that unlocked years of her life. Then she cried as I told her about Frank.

"Your father was a brutal man, Ellen. He did awful things."

"I remember. I'm sorry."

"I always wondered about Frank," she said. "I never trusted him. He was too much like your dad."

I knew women were said to marry their fathers, but I'd never considered Frank a lot like mine. Frank wasn't nearly as charming.

"Are you okay for money?"

I'd never, never, asked my mother for help. "I'm on welfare, Mom," I said.

"I'll put some money in the bank for you. A getaway fund, for if you have to leave the country." I'd told her I was thinking of fleeing if Frank pushed things into court.

"I don't know what to expect," I said. "Carolina keeps saying he's outside with a gun. I try to imagine what he said to her. 'If you tell Mommy, I'll shoot you'? 'It'll kill your mother if you tell her'? Something about guns. A threat involving guns."

"Those poor babies," Mom said.

Meara heard from Frank's attorney, who seemed "unsettled" by the case. He'd advised Frank not to try for contact with the children.

It was good news. It made me feel safer to know Frank wasn't hunting us and I could loosen my vigilance. Not that I'd be able to, really: looking over my shoulder was habitual.

I thought how I had got little out of reporting that I could not have got on my own. Physical safety, maybe. Bits of therapy. Against all our losses.

Amy's diet was not improving. I'd get guardedly hopeful—she'd eat a biscuit, she'd eat a tiny sliver of ham—but then she'd shut down again. She was now fourteen months old. I had tricks that would cajole a tree to eat, but they didn't work on Amy. Nothing was getting into her mouth but bottles, her soother, cereal and the odd cracker.

I wished someone could help me with her spells. I now knew what they were properly called—night terrors—but in Vancouver not a single therapist worked with abused babies or with nonverbal kids. I wasn't sure that any of the professionals I spoke with had actually witnessed night terrors. They didn't seem to understand their ferocity, that I *couldn't* settle Amy. I heard censure behind their sympathy: If you only were a better mother ...

The professional attention centred on Carolina, but in many ways Amy seemed more wounded to me. Frank might have led up to assaulting Carolina—first only masturbating around her, say, gradually escalating to touch—allowing Carolina time to develop a sense of self. Amy, on the other hand, so soon assaulted—at two weeks, I guessed, the time when her personality had changed—had had no chance. Of the two, she was the more fragile, the more broken. I could only hope there was healing in her unlimited expression of trauma. There was that: Amy lived her abuse over and over. Ultimately, might that be soothing?

I overheard a little girl from downstairs tell a little boy, "Don't go upstairs 'cause Carolina will pull down your pants and play doctor with you."

Carolina said, "What do you do with your therapist, Mommy?"

"Mostly I talk," I said, "about my family. My mommy and daddy and how it felt to have my daddy hurt me." It was my first reference to my own sexual abuse since our stay at the transition house; I felt queasy bringing it up, fearful of saddling Carolina with more.

"I thought it was my fault when my dad hurt me," Carolina said.

"Yeah, that's what I thought, too, when I was little. I didn't know it was my dad's fault."

"But it doesn't feel better to talk about it. It feels worse."

"Does it?"

"I thought you and your therapist talked about what a bad girl I am."

I assured her we didn't. I stroked her hair while the sorrow inside me built like tinder, dry and flammable.

I was deeply lonely. Sometimes I called Brigit, but though she set up times to see me, she always cancelled them later with some or other weak excuse and eventually I gave up.

Something was hardening inside me, growing colder. I rarely burst into tears the way I had for the first couple of weeks; in fact, I couldn't cry, not even in therapy. It was less humiliating that way, but I wasn't sure it was progress. Instead of crying

I was building a protective shell. Under it was a vast cacophony of emotion, a muddy swirl of conflicting, vulnerable feelings I couldn't afford to let out.

But alone at night, after Carolina and Amy were sleeping, I felt those feelings stir and knock up against me like fists. I had hours of panic to push back, hours of repetitious memories of my father to squelch. I felt I'd be trampling the same territory forever.

I was two years old, holding my father's high hand. Skinned rabbits dangled from the rafters. Kids, he'd compared them to; kids who hadn't behaved.

As I relived this, I could feel the child I'd been shrinking, getting lost. The loss of innocence. The loss of my father as a haven. Everything that came later was a construct: girls who had lurched into being to replace the original one, girls who could do what was required.

The girl I was at eight, when I'd "seduced" my father's friends.

I called Constable Mills to tell him what Carolina had said about sucking her father's penis.

"Did Carolina indicate on which dates that occurred?"

The futility of our legal fight hit home hard.

"Carolina," he repeated, "did she give you dates and times?"

"No, Constable," I answered wearily. "She did not."

What did I want? Frank charged? Yes. Carolina to face him in court? No. Frank convicted? Yes. I wanted the police to make Frank stop. That's all. I didn't care how.

Little raped Suzanne downstairs, temporarily made a ward of the court so that social services could deny her father access, lost her case. Despite her stitches, she was ordered back to her dad.

Amy was hell on wheels, into everything. She'd learned to climb and she was a one-baby destructo unit on a seek and destroy mission. She drove me to the ends of the earth. She ripped books. She tore my journals. She threw food. She discovered her excrement, a sort of always-available finger paint, and I spent hours wiping shit off walls and cupboards, off furniture. One lovely morning she painted herself, hair and all. To get the slick, stinking, noxious stuff off her required five baths; my stomach heaved.

"If a boy and a little girl made a baby, that would be very bad, right?" Carolina asked.

"Well," I answered, "they can't."

"Even though they can't, I sure want to." She bit her nails. "I wouldn't like it, though." She pulled Blankie over her head.

Meara asked Frank's lawyer for custody, no access for six months, voluntary therapy for Frank, $350 a month in child support and the return of some of my belongings. She felt that there was more than enough evidence to obtain a restraining order against Frank; she advised his lawyer that if Frank made an application for access, the Ministry of Human Resources would apprehend the girls under the Family and Child Services Act.

When Meara told me that my children, like Suzanne downstairs, could be apprehended, I was shocked.

"How else could the ministry protect them?" Meara said. "Think about it. If Frank were awarded access, Ellen, how else could they stop him from seeing them?"

It was logical; it protected my children. But I still felt cold way down deep.

Notice back from Frank's lawyer agreed to my retaining custody, to child support and the return of my things. But Frank wanted to negotiate the interval of no contact and refused to seek therapy, which he saw as an admission of guilt. Interestingly, his lawyer wanted to know if there were allegations with respect to Amy, and I could not decipher what this meant. Did it mean that Frank was expecting some? His lawyer said there was "more to the situation" than was obvious; we were acting as if Frank and only Frank could have committed the abuse.

Had anyone ever thought, I wondered, shaking the lawyer's letter at Meara, of the extraordinary idea of blaming the crime on the criminal?

We moved. By September second we were ensconced in a top-floor, city-view, one-bedroom, roach-infested apartment after two months in frustrating—but safe—shelters.

I finished my six weeks of sessions with Gloria. My group for mothers ended. But luckily I found a therapist whose fee scale slid to one dollar, and I went to see her once a week. Her name was Elaine, and for the first time I began doing work that helped me. With Elaine, cracks began to appear in my armour.

Joyce, the young woman assigned to give Carolina "therapy," returned to town. Though I didn't want to seem uncooperative, I didn't trust her. Still, when Carolina balked at seeing her, I said all the right things. That Joyce was there to help her. That anything Carolina said or did while she was with Joyce was confidential. That unless Carolina requested it, Joyce wouldn't tell me anything. Carolina knew I was snowing her, though. She refused to go.

I knew it would look bad for me, but I called Joyce.

"I thought this would happen," she said smugly. "I assumed she'd pull away after what happened at Lowther House."

"What are you talking about?" I said, anger barrelling through me. "Are you saying that Carolina disclosed to you?"

"Oh, yes. She drew a picture of her father hurting her, and she was very angry. Remember when she bit that other child? She'd just talked about how unfair it was to be punished for biting her father. I think Frank spanked her after she bit his penis."

I dreamed I was at my ex-landlord's house explaining to his wife what had happened. Frank burst in. I said, "Why did you do it?" and he stared at me. I held up a tape recorder. "See?" I said. "It's turned off. I won't tell anyone. Why, Frank?"

Extremely slowly, he answered, "I don't know."

When I woke I understood that at bottom I just didn't get it. I had all the analysis. I understood that rape was a crime of power acted out in a sexual arena. But I didn't understand *why*. That Frank wouldn't either, that Frank would be bewildered by what he had done, made a sort of bizarre sense.

Carolina woke up screaming. I carried her into the bathroom for a pee and held her sleepy and whimpering on the toilet. When I let go of her to get toilet paper, she trembled and yelled. "What is it, honey? What is it?" I asked, but she couldn't say. I could hear Amy crying too. I carried Carolina, shrieking, back into the bedroom. She clung to me. She wouldn't let me put her down.

Finally she said, "Oh, Mama," in a lost, end-of-the-world voice. "Oh, Mama, we weren't supposed to move from Lowther House." She swivelled her head between the window and her bedroom door as though frightened someone would burst in. Finally she lay down and went back to sleep.

The next morning she was a horror. I'd hardly slept and I was upset, terrified, worried about money, sad about my friends and heartbroken about my father. When I told Carolina we were out of Cheerios, she shouted, "I won't live here! I won't love you! I hate you! You're a bad mommy, a stupid dumb old mommy. I hope you fall down and hurt yourself, you stupid mommy."

I yelled back. "Go to your room, Carolina, this instant. Get in your room *now*!" I intimidated her, moving close and showing her my height. Carolina skedaddled. I wanted to wring her little neck.

She came out while I was trying to tempt Amy with Rice Krispies and said, "Daddy won't do it again, you know."

I looked sideways at her, still angry. Sarcastically, I said, "Oh? Why not?"

"Because he's my daddy. And besides, the police told him he couldn't."

Instantly, I melted. "Things got pretty bad when you told, didn't they, Carolina? No more Daddy, no more Sammy, an upset mommy, transition house. You must think telling caused all the bad things. But it didn't."

"I want you to tell the police Daddy won't do it again."

"I'd like your daddy to tell you it was all his fault and he'll never do it again," I said. Amy had her hands in her bowl; she was squeezing her fists around the cereal. Gently I explained that Frank hadn't told the police what he'd done. When the police asked him if he'd done any bad touching, he'd said no.

Carolina erupted. "That's a lie! That's a huge lie! I'm going to tell them he's a liar. I'm going to tell them that lie is as big as a policeman's arms spread out."

I winced.

"Daddy scares me all the time," Carolina said. "He put milk in my vagina, Mommy."

I looked from Carolina to the milk jug on the table. I thought she was inventing. "Oh, you're just kidding."

"People who put milk in vaginas are as bad as the whole world and daddies are as bad as the whole world."

Precipitously, I thought: Milk. Vagina. Semen? My stomach churned.

Constable Mills wasn't in, so I called Roma Flagge and recounted my conversation with Carolina about the police. Roma was disgusted with me. According to her, I had given Carolina "too much information." Carolina didn't need to know that the police didn't believe her, she said.

"I didn't say the police didn't believe her, Roma! I only told her her father said he hadn't hurt her."

"That's too much for you to tell her, that he lied."

"*She* said he lied, not me," I retorted, but I was fighting a losing battle. In the ministry's eyes, I could do nothing right.

I was too pissed off to mention Carolina's disclosure about milk, and I vowed never to confide in the ministry again.

After I read that gonorrhea was one cause of gagging in young children, I had my G.P. take a swab of Amy's throat. I knew the shit would hit the fan if the ministry found out. I was supposed to do only what they recommended, and they'd see this as another example of "overreaction." But none of them had witnessed one of Amy's spells. I didn't really think that Amy could be infected, considering that Carolina and I had no symptoms, but I needed the assurance of test results. If it turned out in the future that Amy *did* have gonorrhea, gone unchecked, I'd want to die.

I convinced Carolina to see Joyce by promising I wouldn't leave the room. I knew how this would probably sit with Joyce, me as "overinvolved," but I also knew that I could not, in good conscience, force Carolina into a situation that scared her, not even to please the ministry. As I was driving her over, Carolina gave me a "what does Mom remember" quiz.

"I told you lots more on Saturday, Mom, remember what?"

"You told me Daddy put milk in your vagina, honey," I said, each word a pulled tooth, a stab. "And that Daddy lied to the police."

"No, Mommy, you don't remember. I also said I wanted to call the police."

"Do you?"

She said righteously, "Yes, I do."

I wasn't sure what to do. Instinct warned me off. I said, "We'll see, all right? We'll talk about it later." I thought of the family photo Carolina had found earlier in the day, how she had thrust it in my face and said, "Here's the *whole* family and Amy was real little. And here's Frank who hurt me."

Frank, I'd thought, not Daddy.

Carolina had pointed to Amy. "She hates her daddy, you know."

We parked at the neighbourhood house. "Alley up," I instructed the girls. "We're here."

My mother told me on the phone that neither my brother Laurence nor my sister Margaret believed that my father had abused me or that Frank had abused the girls.

I got a call from a woman I'd met at transition house. Her eight-year-old daughter had disclosed that her father had wrapped her head in a sound-muffling towel, bent her over the toilet and raped her. The little girl had genital herpes.

I contacted my old friend Teresa. Had she heard what was going on? I asked. Oh, yes, she'd heard, she said, her voice tight and distant. "Frank hasn't been charged," she went on protectively. "If anything had happened, Ellen, the police would have charged him. You're just being cruel."

I was quiet. Finally I said, "Do something for me, will you? One thing. Just be careful with your kids."

"I trust Frank," she said. "Why'd you do this to him?"

But I was already hanging up.

My sister called. During our stilted conversation, Carolina wandered out of the bedroom, scared of mice and monsters. I ran my litany: "It's okay, sweetheart. Nothing's going to get you, nothing's—"

"'Cept Daddy!" she cried and ran back to bed.

Margaret was skeptical about Frank's abuse of the kids, but she told me two things that interested me: Frank had made repeated passes at her; he'd mentioned to her that he'd slept with a co-worker of mine. I learned there'd always been a covert side to Frank.

"Mom," said Carolina, holding *Where Did I Come From?*, "this sperm is yellow."

"Uh-huh?"

"Sperm is not yellow. It's white, Mom, and sort of gloppy see-through."

Carolina asked Bill next door—I'd struck up a friendship with his wife, Cory—if he would hurt her if she showed him her private parts. When he said, "No, never," she seemed reassured.

Cory overheard Carolina on a play phone, saying, "Dad, if I see you again will I be safe?"

And Carolina said to Cory's daughter, Sheyelle, "You have to watch this movie. It's okay. There's no fathers in it."

Sheyelle said, "Why no fathers?"

"Because fathers hurt you."

"Bill doesn't," Sheyelle replied.

I was grateful Carolina had a good male role model in her life, grateful she got to hear that not all men hurt their daughters.

"Mom," Carolina asked, "sex is a pain and tickle, right?"

"For grownups it's just a tickle," I answered.

"No, Mommy, it's always a pain and bad, bad, bad. Even when I get to be a million, I won't like it."

"It's always up to you, Carolina," I said. "When you grow up, you can decide whether or not you want to have sex. No one has to."

Carolina pulled up her nightie and exposed her bottom. "Don't you think my bum is funny?"

"Ordinary," I said, "like anyone's bum. Just a normal bum."

"Even like Daddy's?"

I didn't reply.

I received a letter from Meara informing me that if Frank's lawyer did not respond to our new correspondence by the end of October, we'd take Frank to court. We'd asked again for an agreement on paper that included no contact for six months. I was terror-stricken.

Carolina began talking about jail, about how kids could go to jail if they'd been bad. I explained that only adults went to jail.

"Well, Frank hurt Amy and me!"

"Do you want Daddy to go to jail?"

"No, that's why I never told anyone."

"Daddy wouldn't go to jail, I don't think, pumpkin. They'd just make sure he never hurt you again."

"My daddy's *all* bad. I like to be hurt. Mommy, Dad said if I was bad he'd go boom, boom, boom in my private parts."

Sometimes I wanted to tape her mouth shut.

Carolina slammed her hand against her crotch, which was festering again, and screamed, "Oww! Oww!"

She told me she'd dreamed she put Amy in a plastic bag and couldn't get her out. That Amy was in a trumpet that fell into water and then a fire.

I mentioned to Carolina that her bangs needed cutting and she said, "Yeah, then Daddy won't know who I am." Then she added, conspiratorially, "Bill's about to do it to me, you know, Mommy."

At a secondhand store along Kingsway, a six-lane street bisecting Vancouver, I lost Amy. She'd been hiding under racks of clothes; when I turned around she was gone. I stared at the closed door, the doorknob. Doorknobs were her latest success.

The store was around a bend in the road, a blind bend, and as I ran out I heard the squeal of brakes, then saw Amy, toddling happily, inches from car bumpers. She saw me and began to run, laughing. Everywhere in me was the sound of brakes, the smell of rubber, the soundless open mouths of motorists. I ran and caught her up as she reached the median.

She could have died. That's all I could think for days: Amy could have died. That I had her, in my arms, in her crib, seemed the most generous of miracles.

15

WORD CAME THAT Frank definitely would not face criminal charges, due to lack of evidence and a reluctance to allow Carolina in court.

I called Barry again. Another disheartening conversation, me wary, Barry angry and cold. He told me that he and Frank were now renting workshop space together. Teresa was allowing Frank to babysit their children, he added. I was stunned—Teresa was using the bodies of her kids to convince Frank he was trusted.

Later I learned from Meara that Frank, unable to deny Carolina's abuse, had accused Barry.

I thought of Barry's loyalty to Frank, of Teresa's, of my brother's. They should have known better. They should have known I was incapable of a smear campaign.

Yet I also knew that, in their shoes, I would have felt the same way. If Teresa had made an allegation against Barry regarding Samantha, when I knew and admired Barry, when I'd taken him in my arms and loved him, I wouldn't have believed her.

But would I have bet my children's well-being on it?

I read a book on sexual abuse prevention to Carolina. It said that mothers sometimes don't believe their children. Carolina asked, "Why? Why don't mommies believe their kids?"

"Because it's hard to imagine that daddies would do stuff like that."

"Oh, yes, they would," Carolina told me angrily. Then she stuck out her bottom lip. "Can I sleep with you?"

"Carolina, you know you can't. I don't get any sleep if you're in the bed. You kick."

"I could sleep with Dad," she said, not for the first time. "I *had* to."

"Why?"

"'Cause my bed had no blankets, Mommy. He said you were supposed to wash them and make my bed and I couldn't sleep in my room till you did."

After moving to the mountain, Frank had taken care of his own laundry. "Didn't he say you kicked?"

"No, he liked it."

"Because he liked touching you, Carolina?"

"Yes, he did. He never complained. Usually I tried to sleep 'cause sometimes I couldn't feel his touching if I was asleep."

I was quiet. Then I grinned and said, "Well, pumpkin, this grownup likes to sleep alone." And nuzzled her neck.

I could no longer have sex with Denise. I didn't feel good about lying beside her, spurning her advances, and I didn't have anything lucid to tell her about reasons. But when she was making love to me, I catapulted back into memories of my father. I couldn't stay connected. I recognized this as a long-term sexual problem, that once the newness of a lover wore off, I was always distant, but it was the first time that I'd stopped because of it, or that memories had followed in the wake. A touch, a smell, a sensation across my skin and I'd be jolted into memory, wrenching away as if Denise had hurt me, crawling to the side of the bed and piling pillows around myself, resenting her.

This response was particular to my partner being a woman, I thought. With men, I'd gone cold but continued with gusto.

Making love with a woman required more of me, all of me; it was a circumstance in which it was impossible to hide.

One Saturday when we were in my bed together and I had refused Denise, cautious about beginning what I'd muck up partway through, she pulled the bottle of wine she'd been drinking from into bed and swigged from it, saying she was sick of this, what did I want anyhow?

"I'm not a machine you can turn off!" she cried, drinking deeply.

"I'm sorry," I murmured, reaching to touch her wrist. "I don't know what's wrong with me."

She jerked away, saying she was going home. She lurched from bed and tugged on her jeans. Though she'd always had a lot to drink when we were together, it had never crossed my mind until now that she had a problem, that she'd probably driven the hour's drive home falling-down drunk more than once.

"Don't go," I said desperately. "Come back to bed," I patted the sheet.

Denise twisted to face me. "If you think I'm staying ...," she started, her glance falling to my breasts and then reluctantly pulling back to my face, "... you're out of your mind. I deserve more than this." She grabbed the neck of the now-empty wine bottle and swung the bottle around.

"Come back to bed, Denise." I tried to plant a come-hither look on my face. Seeing that she was going to break, that her arousal was still foremost in her mind, I put my hands on my breasts, my fingers on my nipples. Moments later, Denise returned to bed, her jeans dangling from one foot, and I reached for her. As long as I was the one doing things, I was safe enough, and when that part was over, Denise fell asleep like a rock. I jerked the sheet up to cover her, disgusted with both of us.

I shopped at secondhand stores since I had little money to buy the girls Christmas gifts; welfare would increase my December cheque by only $25 a child. Frank had our box of decorations, including stockings my mother had made the kids, so in mid-November I blew nearly a hundred dollars on replacements. I knew it was a way of minimizing Frank's power over us; if I did not think how Frank had all our Christmas tree ornaments, how Frank had their stockings, I was less sad.

I received notice that Frank wanted access beginning January first—his lawyer pointed out that that gave me the six months of no access I'd wanted—and that, additionally, he wanted a Christmas visit with the girls.

Carolina, Amy, how am I going to keep you safe? I thought wildly.

Carolina's last appointment with Joyce ended with Joyce shaking her by the shoulders in the lobby—I walked in on them—and shouting, "You have to talk to me, you have to talk!" I was appalled and pulled Carolina roughly from her grasp.

I began to take Carolina to Elaine.

Amy's gonorrhea swab came back negative.

I had to prepare Carolina for the possibility she'd soon see her father. I told her gently what lawyers were and that we'd received a letter from Frank's.

She said, "Does Daddy know where we live?"

I assumed Frank did, but I told her no. "Daddy says it was Barry who hurt you."

"Barry never hurt me. He never did! Daddy's wrong. Daddy hurt me. Give me the number of the police!" She was frantic, twisting around the room. Then she said, "Daddy never hurt me. I'll go up to the mountain, but not overnight."

"Look," I said. "I know your father hurt your private parts, Carolina. I also know you want to forget all about it. So we can forget about it and still know it happened, okay?"

"Okay," she said happily. "It really did happen but now we're forgetting about it! I'll go up to the mountain for twenty days with *you*, then I'll stay alone. I'll tell you if he hurts me."

"The visit is just Christmas afternoon for a couple of hours at a restaurant, honey."

"We could sew his fingers!"

"What?"

"Yeah, sew his fingers!"

"I don't understand."

"His fingers would be too big to fit!"

I closed my eyes, too sad to speak.

"I just want him to stop hurting me, that's all."

"I know," I said quietly, "oh, boy, do I know."

Carolina woke me the night after I took her to a Raffi concert. She'd dreamed she was in a skating rink change room, wearing no top. There were men taking photographs of her. She said, "I was almost crying when I woke up, Mom."

She said, "If Daddy stayed overnight, it would be okay if his penis went inside me while I was asleep and he was asleep."

She said, "Mom, would Raffi ever hurt me?" Then, sleepily, "Mom? You can do anything you want to me when I'm asleep. But not touch my private parts."

I called Barry again. He said, "You had two men in your life and got rid of us both, Ellen. It couldn't be more transparent."

"He's accusing *you*, though, Barry," I sputtered.

"Ellen," he said thinly, "wake up. Can't you see what you're doing?"

Meara refused the Christmas visit and the January access request. I waited on pins and needles: would it force Frank into court?

Back and forth, the lawyers fenced. Meara obtained a mid-January appointment with the ministry to have the information in my files released to her, preparatory to a court battle. Frank's lawyer agreed to wait to hear what our side had. I was jubilant to hear that the proceedings would be stalled over the holidays.

Carolina worried that Frank would arrive disguised as Santa Claus or with Santa Claus, sneaking in through the patio door she wanted me to leave cracked open in the absence of a chimney.

Amy, at a year and a half, had a full set of teeth pushed askew by her soother until the inch gap between top and bottom made it impossible for her to speak intelligibly.

Denise called drunk one night in mid-December, slurrily telling me she'd met a man and was remarrying before the end of the year.

"Congratulations," I said. My throat was dry and scratchy, but I managed to say what she wanted to hear, even if I said it in a pinched, sarcastic voice.

Denise rambled on about Ryan, the man she'd met when she took her VCR in for repairs, and finally I said, "Denise! A man!" She was bisexual, she said, and what was it, did I have something against men? That was it, wasn't it? I begrudged her her happiness.

"But you just met him!"

"He makes me happier than you ever could," Denise wobbled out, laughing.

"Oh, Denise," I said, "don't. I love you." I felt tears well in my eyes. I'd never said I loved her before. But faced with the prospect of losing her, I thought it was true.

"*Ryan* loves me," Denise said thickly. I heard her take a long drink.

"I'm glad for you," I forced myself to say.

"You'd better be," she said. Then she got an idea. "We'll have you to dinner, that's it. Come for dinner the day after Christmas. Boxing Day."

"Sure," I said.

"You're happy for me, right? You're really happy for me?"

"Oh, Denise," I said.

"Say it."

I swallowed and said it, then said it three more times before she was satisfied.

Gifts arrived at Carolina's daycare, delivered by Dennis, Frank's brother. Carolina hadn't seen him, thank God, and I got the box home without her noticing. I opened it late on Christmas Eve, carefully unwrapping each gift. Many of the gifts were ordinary and benign: a Fisher Price doctor's kit, a crib mobile for Amy. But there was a Mickey Mouse hat and T-shirt for Carolina, Frank's way, I guessed, of letting Carolina know I'd kept her from a trip to Disneyland.

There were intricately crafted wooden jewellery boxes I recognized as made by Barry and, in each, a horoscope. My breath caught as I read Carolina's. In Frank's handwriting, it said, "You have a weakness for the opposite sex."

In another note, inside a third jewellery box addressed to me, Frank had written, "This box should be filled with coal for you have been a very BAD girl this year! Santa."

Then I unwrapped a framed, nude photo of the girls in the bathtub. On the back it said, "All I have are the memories and a few pictures. Hope you are happy, Ellen." I was struck dumb and tossed the photo as if it had burned me.

A card of a woman in lingerie bending over daisies said, "Ellen, this card reminds me of the beauty both inward and outward that you possessed. The outward beauty may still be there but judging from your actions your heart has turned to stone. Still, Frank." There was a postscript that heartened me: "P.S.," it said, "have a nice life." I hoped it meant that Frank planned to leave us alone for good.

It was two o'clock Christmas morning. I sat surrounded by tattered wrapping paper, the tree lit, a plate of cookies and a glass of eggnog on the table, my children asleep, my head in my hands.

At seven, Carolina woke me whispering about Santa. I wanted to be cheerful for her; I wanted to take pleasure in her excitement, but as I folded up my bed and woke and changed Amy, I felt pulverized by loneliness. I watched my daughters open gifts, watched the pile of bright wrappings strewn about the living room grow, and ached. Mom called, but I received her greetings hollowly.

I wanted the day to be over. I gave the girls the gifts Frank had sent, minus the creepy ones, wrapped in brown grocery bags I had painted with Carolina's poster paints. On the tags I had written, "Love, Santa."

I left Frank's tag on one gift. When Carolina opened it to find a puzzle of kittens she looked up at me. "Oh," she cried, flinging it from her, "I thought it would be poisoned candies!"

One night early in January, as I was tucking Carolina in, I suggested she remove the sweater she had on over her nightie.

She clambered up and took it off. "If you get too hot, Mom, you die."

"Oh, no," I said, amused. "Not from a sweater. You only sweat from a sweater."

"Can you die in a fire, Mom, can you? Can you die *in* a fire or just with fire?"

"Well," I said, "in, I guess. But it's not something to worry about. There's hardly ever a fire that's dangerous."

"You can die with fire, right?"

"No," I said, though I couldn't imagine what "with fire" meant.

"Just *in* fire?"

"Yes," I said, giving in.

She crawled into bed. She turned over and said, her voice hollow and stricken, "I guess Daddy didn't know that." Instantly, she fell off to sleep.

During one of Amy's spells, Carolina turned to me and said, "I think she's thinking about Dad. Know why? 'Cause at the mountain she says, 'Mama, Mama,' when Dad hurts her."

My heart twisted.

"She saw Dad hurt me."

"Oh, yeah?" I asked cautiously.

"Yeah. She was crying." Carolina swung her legs into the air. "My crotch smells yucky, Mom. I'm afraid other people will think so too. My arms and legs are tied up."

They weren't. "Uh-huh?"

"I do it in case someone wants to tie me up."

"Practise?"

"Yeah."

"I don't think I'd like to be tied up," I said carefully.

"Me either. I just do it in case." Then she said, "Where did the first man and woman come from? Did someone wave a magic wand?"

Then, "Mom, the air is not as fresh as everyone thinks. It's been around a long time."

Then, "Mom, I'm mad even when I'm happy, 'cause of Dad. You are too."

Finally, tired of Carolina's chatter, I sent her from the room and closed the door so I could calm Amy.

When I came out, Amy restored and cuddly, Carolina was in tears. Her little face tilted up to ask, "Why did you close the door?"

"Just so I could help Amy get over her crying, pumpkin. Why, did it frighten you?"

Carolina peered at me. "I thought you told me to leave so you could abuse Amy."

I looked at the Barbie doll she was playing with. Its limbs were bound.

I was always looking over my shoulder. Frank could appear at any moment, I thought. This central scare: Frank could appear. I supposed it had to do with the years of private detectives my father had hired to watch my mother. All through my teen-age years, men skirted the parameters of my life, spying from cars behind bushes, hoping to obtain evidence that Mom was having a sexual life. That way Dad could stop paying alimony.

In talking to the ministry, Meara found out that Frank had told the police Carolina had seen us making love; she never had. He'd said she'd been traumatized during Amy's birth. He'd said Carolina had continually tried to fellate him and that he'd repeatedly had to push her from his lap.

"Mom," Carolina said, appearing from her bedroom one night after I'd tucked her in. "Daddy hurt my genitals at the mountain."

I was preoccupied, sitting up in bed writing in my journal. I made a noise of acknowledgement.

"He took pictures of me," she went on.

Frank's infernal camera, I thought distractedly, still not paying Carolina very much mind.

"Of my privates, Mom. He made me drink yucky stuff, then he tied me to the bed, Mommy, and he took pictures of me. Then he lit the ends of the rope on fire."

It moved in me like gas, like an explosion. What had I just heard? My journal fell to the floor. "What did you just say? Say that again."

"I thought I was going to burn up, Mommy."

Her fears of fire, I thought, her endless games of bondage. Be cool, I thought. Don't overreact.

Carolina was shaking. It was warm in the apartment but Carolina, her blue eyes deep and endless in her small face, was trembling. My sofa bed was opened out. I pulled Carolina up and into my arms and held her mutely.

I thought of calling Constable Mills again, of demanding the police search Frank's cabin for pornographic photographs of Carolina. But they hadn't once acted like I was in my right mind. I'd go it alone. I'd protect the girls myself. There was a spot inside me that had suddenly gone dead and cold and hard and determined. It bypassed emotion. Frank, I thought, if this is true, you are a dead man. If this is true, I will kill you.

I didn't respond to Carolina; she fell asleep in my arms and I carried her to bed and stood over her, watching her sleep, not thinking, just watching.

That night, I woke from dreams where Carolina and Amy were only torsos gushing blood, where Frank stalked and stole the children, where Carolina lay splayed on the bed on which she had been born, tethered and burning.

Something had ended. I was now an adversary. No more lawyer games, I thought. No more social workers.

And this unshakeable thought: No more Frank.

Ever.

The restaurant I chose was the same one where, months earlier, I had met with Roma.

Denise's new husband Ryan held open the door. He was a cheerful bear of a man, and I smiled tightly up at him. He and Denise and I had managed to establish some kind of friendship, and they had agreed to sit at a table across the restaurant, watching to see I wasn't hurt.

I didn't know if what I was doing was smart. After I sat down, ordering only coffee, I kept turning around to make sure that Denise and Ryan were in view.

Then I forced myself to take deep, slow breaths. I checked my watch; I checked inside my purse. I was waiting for Frank.

Frank had been given a court date to fight me for access to Carolina and Amy, Meara had told me apologetically. We'd "fought the good fight," she'd said, and reminded me it had been nearly a year since I'd found out about the abuse, a year in which I'd kept my daughters safe.

"So?" I said.

Now I had to accomplish one last thing. Sweat was breaking out on my palms and snaking between my breasts.

I reminded myself of Carolina's disclosures. I wanted them fresh and real behind my eyes. I made the picture of Carolina drugged, of Frank lighting on fire the ends of the rope he'd used to tie her up.

This one last thing, I told myself, breathing hard.

When Frank opened the door, I felt dizzy. When he saw me, he nodded. He pulled out the chair across from me and lowered himself into it, long, leggy and as handsome as ever. His hair was shorter and he was clean-shaven, but he looked like the same Frank I'd always known.

"How are you?" I asked softly.

He shrugged.

I sat back, reached into my purse and pushed a button on the recorder I'd brought. "I've been concerned about you," I said, not untruthfully.

I heard anger in his tone as he asked what I wanted.

I waded in. "You've set a court date, and I want to discuss that."

Frank blinked, surprised. "How are the girls?"

His question gave me the road in that I needed. I began to answer honestly, telling Frank about Carolina's and Amy's ongoing symptoms. I leaned towards him as I spoke, punctuating my words with my hands. I told him that Carolina's therapy had barely begun, that no one, yet, would consider seeing Amy. It was going to be arduous, I said. Finally I told him how I understood this wasn't something that had happened *just* to Carolina and Amy. It had happened to him, too.

But if he took us to court, I said, I'd be forced to use the opportunity to bring forward the doctor's report, the child abuse report, therapists' reports and the police report. I told him I had dozens of affidavits from friends who'd heard disclosures from Carolina.

"I want you to know that I'll fight you tooth and nail."

Frank didn't try to interrupt.

"I know," I continued, "that you understand this isn't a vendetta. This is what I have to do to protect the girls." After considering a moment, I added, "And so should you, as their father. You should protect them from yourself."

Frank slowly nodded.

"All right?" I raked my fingers through my hair. "That's understood?"

He nodded again.

Talking to Frank had always been like pulling teeth. I said, "Okay, then, one last thing… "

Frank glanced quickly around the restaurant.

I stared directly into his eyes. "Why did you do it, Frank? Why did you rape Carolina and Amy?"

I passionately wanted to know. Suddenly, that's all I wanted, to know why.

Frank lowered his eyes. Then, looking directly at me, he leaned forward.

My mouth was dry.

Frank wiped his hand over his forehead. He subsided into his chair. Slumped over, with shame skirting his face, he told me, "I don't know."

It was exactly what he'd said long ago in one of my dreams. I could hardly believe its inadequacy. When my surprise wore off, I said, "You'll leave us alone? Give us the time we need to heal?"

Frank shrugged.

"Do the right thing, Frank," I urged. I pushed up and stood above him, signalling an end to our meeting. I offered him my hand.

Slowly, he stood, too, and took my hand between both of his.

"Take care of yourself," I said.

"I'm sorry," he said, meeting my eyes. Then he dropped my hand and turned to go.

He was dressed as he usually was, in a plaid flannel shirt and blue jeans. He didn't look back. Instead, pushing open the restaurant door, Frank Moore, Carolina and Amy Moore's father, walked out of our lives.

≈

PART THREE

IN CHOOSING A PLACE to end this book, I chose randomly. Because, while it's true that after that evening in the restaurant I never saw or heard from Frank again and have not the foggiest idea what happened to him, Carolina went on spilling her alarming utterances, and Amy, in her inarticulate way, eventually added her own. I, of course, had years ahead before my own memories would cease to torment me.

All of the names in my story have been changed. It protects the misguided and Frank, but primarily it protects my children. They're big enough to say. And they say No, no real names. We know it's important to do this, Mom, but no real names.

Frank in the book is as close to the real Frank as I could make him. I really am Ellen. None of the situations I described are made up. Some of them were humiliating for me to write about, but I tried not to fudge, to make Frank look worse or me better. Carolina's dialogue with me after June 1982, recorded as it happened, is put down here verbatim. For simplicity's sake I've often squashed several conversations into one, but I didn't alter the words. Some identifying details are changed, like what Frank did for a living and where we resided.

Even in those first, terrible months, the girls and I had regular times and fun times and hard times that had nothing to do with abuse. Eventually we lived a life that was only 50 per cent abuse-centred. Then 30 per cent. Then 10 per cent. For years now it's been about 5 per cent. The other 95 per cent of the time, we're having an ordinary life. Like anyone's.

I don't want to whitewash things. Ordinary doesn't mean easy. There are still days when I'm overwhelmed by the challenge of parenting abused kids, and there are hundreds of days like that behind me. All the practical problems I have, like poverty that was for years so severe it forced us into food bank lines, and ill health (I had, in a nine-month span, a diagnosis of cervical cancer and a heart attack that left me disabled), make all the ordinary things extra hard.

I have never gotten to perfect. I work on the "good enough" plan. The kids have "good enough" shoes. "Good enough" food. "Good enough" parenting.

In 1984, I applied for and won a Criminal Injury Compensation Award. This means that the evidence submitted on my behalf—from the doctor, the police and the social workers involved—supported my claim of Frank's sexual abuse. Practically, this means that I don't have to pay for therapy for the girls.

So, it's some easier now.

But there were plenty of bone-cold years when it wasn't, years full of illness, exhaustion and depression.

One afternoon in 1983, when I was taking training to work with survivors of childhood sexual abuse, I brought a bag of anatomically correct dolls into the living room with me. I began working on lecture notes at my desk. Amy, then two, pulled the dolls from the bag and undressed them. I watched with a half-eye, curious but distracted. When she had the little girl doll and the adult male doll undressed, she laid the girl on her back. She lowered the penis of the male doll into the girl's mouth. She was very deliberate. The penis, made of stuffed cotton, wouldn't fit. Amy concentrated, trying to wiggle the body parts together.

Carolina, five years old, hands on her hips, stood off to the side, frowning and watching her sister. Finally, she stepped forward. "That's *not* how you do it," she proclaimed.

I put down my pen.

Carolina grabbed the male doll from Amy. "This is Daddy. So just put him on his back." Carolina did this, then tore the little girl away. "Now the girl doll's mouth goes on top, like this. See?" She wiggled and pushed till the male doll's penis fit in the little girl doll's mouth. "The girl has to be on top."

Amy had been quiet, watching intently. Now she let loose a string of complaints in her incomprehensible language. Her inflection said Carolina was a boob, that little girls did *not* belong on top.

I thought of Amy's immobility during the abuse. She'd been newborn, and Frank had had to come at her from above.

Amy ripped the dolls from Carolina and reversed things, Daddy doll on top.

"You are *so* stupid, Amy," shouted Carolina. "Mom! Amy's wrong, right? It doesn't go like that, right?"

I thought how Amy was right and how Carolina was right and how life, then, was wrong, unutterably wrong.

Some time later, I read Amy a kids' book on prevention. She sat distracted on my lap. About halfway through I realized her kind of abuse wasn't discussed, so I added a phrase, saying offenders could also put their penises in a child's mouth.

Amy exploded. She slipped off my lap, grabbed her mouth, stretched it and began to scream, "Oww! Oww!" She watched me carefully. I nodded. She made a motion as if she were holding her bottle and thrust something invisible into her mouth. "Hurt!" she cried. "Hurt Amy! Penis! Penis everywhere!" She squirmed, slapping herself on the face and torso and legs. She lay down and tore at her mouth. But it wasn't a spell—she was fully with me, trying to communicate, playing a horrible game of charades.

"It's over, honey," I said. "All gone. Now Amy's safe, you're safe, honey. It wasn't your fault. All gone now."

Eventually she rose and climbed back on my lap. She pointed at the book. She wanted me to finish reading it, so I did.

Elaine, the therapist I had found, saw Carolina for about two years, wrapping her in a fantasy world of protective dragons, before she decided she could start work with Amy, then three. Because Elaine no longer had a sliding scale and my therapy wasn't covered by our award, I saw a psychiatrist who was reimbursed through the provincial medical plan.

At the start of kindergarten, Amy was still verbally incomprehensible, even though her teeth had corrected themselves once she gave up soothers. A speech pathologist worked tirelessly and at home I drilled her in enunciation games. By the beginning of grade one, Amy's speech was intelligible but sounded accented. By the start of grade two, it was normal.

Carolina got breast buds at seven and began menstruating at ten, in grade five, as if her early desire to be grown had installed itself in her pituitary gland.

In the fall of 1989, my friend Teresa, Barry's ex, from whom I'd been seven years estranged because of Frank, was murdered by an unknown assailant.

It sent me into a tailspin. I'd been in hiding for years, registering the girls under assumed last names at school, waiting for Frank. But it wasn't me who got murdered, it was Teresa. She'd been involved in a messy custody dispute with the father of her new baby when it happened.

After her death, I had a mean series of dreams in which Frank stalked us, dreams in which I'd see him cross the street and I'd shout frantically to the kids, "Down! On your hands and knees! Crawl!" Dreams that culminated with Frank breaking open my skull with a fireplace poker.

I got back in touch with Barry after Teresa's death, and Carolina picked up her friendship with Sammy. Barry and I are pretty good friends now. He doesn't believe Frank hurt the kids, but at least he believes *I* believe Frank hurt the kids. His path and Frank's diverged, and he hasn't heard from Frank in years.

I'm still friends with Denise, who has divorced Ryan and come out as a lesbian.

I haven't seen or heard from Brigit, Susan or my brother Laurence.

Amy, in grade seven, remains in therapy with Elaine. She's wild and still pops with anger. Though her spells finally ended when she was about five, she had fierce, fiery temper tantrums more than once a day until she was ten, and things are hardly quiet now—she's often verbally abusive. Her diet has never improved. She's been diagnosed as suffering from post-traumatic stress disorder, the syndrome first diagnosed in Vietnam veterans. There is supposition but not firm diagnosis suggesting she might have multiple personality disorder.

Amy will pass a school test with honours one week and the next, on a very similar test, fail abysmally. Possibly different children write the tests; possibly the quixotic girl I parent is many girls.

Certainly she is chaotic. But in recent months, as Amy abandons her need to diet herself into less than her already frighteningly skinny self, Elaine and I have noticed a change. Amy is starting to respond effectively to her world. Instead of working against herself, she has begun to work in ways that will make her life easier.

Carolina is in eleventh grade, French immersion. She is a poised, intelligent, analytical fifteen, a hypochondriac with an unnerving fascination for fire. She's recently re-entered therapy, which she left years ago, because she's been suffering flashbacks. A year or so ago she told me about having watched from under a table as her father orally raped Amy and about the guilt she felt for hoping that she wasn't next.

And several years ago, without any hint from me, Carolina said, while we were watching a TV program on autism, "Mom? When I was little, you know, when Dad was doing that stuff to me, I almost went autistic."

Quietly, I nodded. I thought back to before Frank and I had separated, when that had been my worry, too.

"I was losing contact with everything. I think I almost went autistic, Mom."

"I thought that myself," I told her, keeping my voice steady.

"And almost had multiple personality."

I hadn't shared Amy's possible diagnosis with her. "Yes," I said, remembering her plastic persona.

"And obsessive-compulsive disorder," she said. She plans to study psychology and astrophysics and reads widely. "Because I had things, rituals. Stuff I had to do. Stuff if I didn't do it, like keep washing my hands over and over, or counting stairs and going up and down them, I'd feel crazy."

"But none of that happened, Carolina."

"No," she said thoughtfully. "It was all just close calls. But I understand those worlds completely. It's like I was there but I came back."

Our fathers had entered us as food, as language, as sleep, sending each of us to the brink of mental illness, then back. But ultimately, ours is a story of resilience, of strength and of love.

I looked at my daughter, then reached to clasp her hand. We sat beside each other acutely aware of the enormous precipices behind us, and the smaller ones still ahead.

≈

AFTERWORD

When I was talking to my daughters about writing this book, I let them know they were welcome to read it. I meant after publication, though, and I was surprised when Carolina read the manuscript sooner—without telling me she was going to. The first I knew of it was when I found this remarkable response on my desk.—E.P.

≈

Mom,
You are beautiful. And your book is beautiful. After reading it, I want my turn. Do with this what you will.

IN READING MY mother's book I found that I have an amazing amount in common with my father. It was enlightening, discovering that I love photography because my father did, I'm quiet because my father was. But as the book progressed, my abuse memories were also triggered.

I have a very clear image of lint in my father's bellybutton. And I remember the snow at his cabin, how ecstatic I was when it was deep enough that I could burrow into it and hide myself.

I recall my mother asking me one morning whether or not my father had hurt me, if he'd touched me in a way he shouldn't have. I was so relieved: it was a glimmer of light in an endless, dark tunnel, bright enough so I could go forward rather than rocking myself into a comfortable world of my own. (Being in that world was safe, though, so safe.) When I saw this light, I seized it between grubby fat fingers and pulled it to me. I had a means of escaping my father. I never loved him. From the beginning there was a cold indifference between us.

Years later, as I began to write poetry and as I talked to my mother, other memories began to wrap me in tentacles. When I read my mother's book I experienced even more. Most of them surfaced randomly. Lately I've been wondering if maybe this is because I created another personality for myself, a personality that knows what I don't, that sometimes just spits memories at me.

My conclusion? My father sexually abused me.

I don't think (right now) that my father ever actually put his penis inside me. I think he mostly used his fingers. This could be why I was so disgusted when I found out a few years ago that people use fingers during sex.

I remember lying in my father's bed, in his cabin, next to him, on his right, with his hand on my crotch. I remember him making me leave so that he could switch to touching my sister. My relief was huge because he wasn't hurting me, but I felt guilt, too, for being unable (unwilling?) to help her.

I did have the eerie fascination with fire my mother describes, although it has decreased now. I've been enraptured by the thought of cannibalism and with the stereotype of being a rebel. I've recently caught myself looking at little boys half my age and thinking of them sexually. I have always possessed a desire to be appalling to people.

My mom says in the book that "sexual abuse is often intergenerational. Survivors of it can grow to love men who mirror the abuser." This statement terrifies me. I've always squirmed when hearing that women tend to fall in love with men who remind them of their fathers. I don't want to fall in love with a man who will violate me (or anyone else). But I've been noticing that the boys I am attracted to have the same quiet, self-oriented, dangerous personality that has been attributed to my father.

Guns still horrify, intimidate and unnerve me. Just before I read my mother's account of my historical fear of them, I had premonitory dreams of being pursued by men with guns. Maybe these dreams represent my current fear of and frustration with sex. Sex scares me. The offers I receive from forty-year-old men on buses ("I want to lick your pussy") scare me. The emotions I experience when making out with a guy scare me. In such situations I've had flashbacks. An example:

I am huddled in a ball at my dad's cabin. The door to the bathroom is right beside me, light shining onto me. The chair I'm under doesn't hide me at all, but I'm too paralyzed by fear to find a better spot. My dad comes in, holding something. I don't know what it is, but it makes me even more scared. He's calling my name softly and menacingly. I know he knows where I am. He pretends not to, raising false hopes he then crushes. Then what? I'm blank about what came next.

My ghosts never really left me. Sometimes they abound. A few months ago I put my "Blankie" (my fourth?) away in my trunk, but I occasionally long to take it back out.

I am the aftermath of my father's misbehaviour.

His actions were not without consequences—although he is no doubt ignorant of them. Approximately ten years of my life were spent depressed. When I was nine and mad at my mom or upset at school, I plotted how to run away—what clothes to take, what food I could squirrel away unnoticed, how I would escape the house. When I was eleven I planned intricate murders of everyone I was mad at. I thought about killing myself—what to leave to whom, how to accomplish the suicide, what my note would say. I'd hold a bottle of aspirin in my hand and wonder how I would get them all down, or hold a pair of scissors and wonder if they were sharp enough to slice open the veins in my wrists. I've been paranoid all my life, anxious, a worry-wart. About *everything.*

It would be simple to teeter into promiscuity. But so far I've chosen chastity.

Being taken advantage of sexually was a violation not only of my physical well-being but also of my mental and emotional privacy and freedom. This betrayal by my father, who was supposed to protect and nurture me, is almost inconceivable.

Two summers ago, with the help of some good and wise friends, I began to understand that I am in control of my emotions— I started to learn how to relax. I learned about loyalty to one's self, about the difference between acceptable and unacceptable compromises. I no longer feel like I live in a hole coated with self-pity and envy. After reading my mother's book, I began seeing a psychologist. I love it. It's wonderful knowing that this woman is there to listen to me talk about myself, that she won't interrupt when I'm talking and won't mind when I interrupt her. I don't always talk about abuse, because that's only one aspect of my life.

Oddly, given a choice, I wouldn't wish the abuse away. Done is done. Nothing is all good or all evil. Good has come of this: learning about acceptance and self-love, friendships with other abuse victims, belief in and empathy for abuse victims, poetry and strength.

My relationship with my mother is nauseatingly healthy. I know of no one who likes and respects their mother as much as I do. I enjoy spending time with her; we have great talks.

Having read my mom's book, I've gotten quite curious about my father—someday I'll confront him. But I don't intend to see him yet; not until I've dealt with this on my own. Now is the time for healing and for having fun.

I'm sure I'll continue to have the occasional emotional crisis. But I am anchored in clear, beautiful water, and a rainbow will always stretch a protective arc over me. I will triumph.

Carolina

WITHDRAWN
LONDON PUBLIC LIBRARIES